THE JOURNAL JURISPRUDENCE VOLUME TWENTY-EIGHT

CONTRIBUTORS

Antonio A. Oposa Jr
University of Hawai'i

Daniele Bertolini
Ryerson University

Gary Lilienthal
Universiti Utara Malaysia

Bronwyn Lay
European Graduate School

Nehaluddin Ahmad
Brunei Darussalam

Laurent Neyret
University of Versailles

Twana A. Hassan
The University of Queensland

Damien Short
University of London

Jasper Doomen
Utrecht University School of Law

Michael Urs Baumgartner
Greenpeace, Switzerland

EDITOR

Dr Aron Ping D'Souza
Stawell Chambers, Melbourne

MICHAELMAS TERM
DECEMBER 2015

Elias Clark

PUBLISHED BY THE ELIAS CLARK GROUP
DISTRIBUTED IN CONNECTION WITH THE GALE GROUP,
A PART OF CENGAGE LEARNING

The Elias Clark Group
www.elias-clark.com

GPO Box 5001
Melbourne, Victoria 3001
Australia

First Published 2015.

Cataloguing-in-Publication entry

Editor: D'Souza, Aron Ping.

Title: The Journal Jurisprudence, Volume Twenty-Eight.

ISBN: 978-0-9925409-8-2 (pbk.)
ISSN: 1836-0955

Subjects: Law – jurisprudence.
Philosophy – general.

This edition may be cited as

(2015) J. Juris.

followed by the page number

Cover Photo:
"Temple hall, Bagan, Myanmar."

Stewart Manley
Lecturer in the Faculty of Law
University of Malaya
Kuala Lumpur, Malaysia

ABOUT THE TYPEFACE

The Journal Jurisprudence is typeset in Garamond 12 and the footnotes are set in Garamond 10. The typeface was named for Claude Garamond (c. 1480 - 1561) and are based on the work of Jean Jannon. By 1540, Garamond became a popular choice in the books of the French imperial court, particularly under King Francis I. Garamond was said to be based on the handwriting of Angelo Vergecio, a librarian to the King. The italics of Garamond are credited to Robert Grandjon, an assistant to Claude Garamond. The font was re-popularised in the art deco era and became a mainstay on twentieth-century publication. In the 1970s, the font was redesigned by the International Typeface Corporation, which forms the basis of the variant of Garamond used in this Journal.

TABLE OF CONTENTS

CALL FOR PAPERS

The field of jurisprudence lies at the nexus of law and politics, the practical and the philosophical. By understanding the theoretical foundations of law, jurisprudence can inform us of the place of legal structures within larger philosophical frameworks. In its inaugural edition, *The Journal Jurisprudence* received many creative and telling answers to the question, "What is Law?" For the second edition, the editors challenged the scholarly and lay communities to inquire into the intersection between jurisprudence and economics.

With the backing of our diverse and disparate community, *The Journal Jurisprudence* has now evolved into a distinct format. We will no longer be setting a question for each issue, but instead designing issues around the articles we received. Therefore, we invite scholars, lawyers, judges, philosophers and lay people to tackle any and all of the great questions of law. Knowing that ideas come in all forms, papers can be of any length, although emphasis is placed on readability by lay audiences.

Papers may engage with case studies, intellectual arguments or any other method that answers philosophical questions applicable to the law. Importantly, articles will be selected based on quality and the readability of works by non-specialists. The intent of the Journal is to involve non-scholars in the important debates of legal philosophy.

The Journal also welcomes and encourages submissions of articles typically not found in law journals, including opinionated or personalised insights into the philosophy of law and its applications to practical situations.

Jurisprudence is published four times per year, to coincide with the four terms of the legal year, in an attractive paperback and electronic edition.

Each author who submits to this volume will be provided with a complimentary copy of the journal.

Length: Any length is acceptable, although readability to non-specialist is key.

Presentation Style: Papers must comply with the Australian Guide to Legal Citations, Second Edition published by the Melbourne University Law Review. An electronic edition is available at, http://mulr.law.unimelb.edu.au/PDFs/aglc_dl.pdf

Submission: You must submit electronically in Microsoft Word format to editor@jurisprudence.com.au. Extraneous formatting is discouraged.

Correspondence can also be sent to this address. If you are considering submitting an article, you are invited to contact the editor to discuss ideas before authoring a work.

SUBSCRIPTION INFORMATION

The Journal is published four times per year in an attractive softcover book. Subscription to the Journal can be achieved by two methods:

1) Single issues can be purchased on amazon.com. Our publishers, the Elias Clark Group, set a retail price for each edition, typically AU$40. However, due to their agreement with amazon.com, the price may vary for retail customers.

2) A subscription to the Journal can be purchased for AU$150 per year, or AU$280 for two years. This price includes postage throughout the world. Payment can be made by international bank cheque, but not a personal cheque, to:

The Journal Jurisprudence,
C/o The Elias Clark Group
GPO Box 5001
Melbourne, Victoria, Australia.

Alternatively, the Journal is available online at www.jurisprudence.com.au and can be read there free of charge.

Taking the Costs of Consent Seriously: An Alternative Understanding of Efficiency As a Legal Concern

Daniele Bertolini
Assistant Professor
Ted Rogers School of Management–Ryerson University
daniele.bertolini@ryerson.ca

Abstract: Most law and economics literature employs efficiency criteria that fit poorly with the structural features of the legal environment. The major limitations trace back to the analytical separation of law from its formative process, which has resulted in an almost exclusive focus on the allocative efficiency of legal entitlements and little or no attention paid to the causal relationship between the efficiency of legal rules and the efficiency of the lawmaking process. I contend that this conventional output-oriented approach is susceptible to the following criticisms: 1) it is affected by logical circularity and/or logical incompleteness; 2) it fails to provide any assurance of increased social welfare, 3) it does not account for the presence of losers, and 4) it does not account for the predictability/adaptivity trade-off associated with legal change.

Based on the foregoing considerations, this paper proposes an alternative understanding of legal efficiency. Efficiency is not an objective property of the outcome independent of the process; rather, it depends on the ability of the law-making process to embody, in a cost-effective manner, the general consensus of all the people concerned. Based on this premise, this paper proposes a methodology focused on the "process-outcome" relationship within the production of law, which I call "process efficiency analysis". It relies on the analytical tools offered by transaction-cost economics and is grounded in the normative principles of constitutional contractarianism. In the last section of the paper, I illustrate process efficiency analysis by using an example from tort law.

Keywords: Pareto Efficiency, Wealth-Maximization, Sources of Law, Law-making Process, Unanimity, Product Liability.

Classification: K00, K40

1. INTRODUCTION

Most law and economics literature employs efficiency criteria that fit poorly with the structural features of the legal environment. The major limitations trace back to the analytical separation of law from its formative process, which has resulted in an almost exclusive focus on the allocative efficiency of legal entitlements and little or no attention paid to the causal relationship between the efficiency of legal rules and the efficiency of the lawmaking process. This paper contends that a promising strategy for overcoming (or mitigating) these shortcomings is to incorporate a transaction-cost analysis of law-making more fully into the analytical perspective developed by the constitutional political economy.

This paper proposes a methodology focused on the "process-outcome" relationship within the production of law, which I call a "process efficiency analysis." It relies on the analytical tools offered by transaction-cost economics and is grounded in the normative principles of constitutional contractarianism. In addition, I contend that a process efficiency analysis is more consistent with the idea of individual consent as a normative basis of efficiency than the conventional output-oriented efficiency criteria.

In economic terminology, the term "efficiency" refers to the idea of Pareto optimality, or, alternatively, to other concepts (such as Kaldhor-Hicks efficiency and social welfare maximization) commonly used in policy analyses to overcome the restricted practicability of the Pareto efficiency criterion. Legal economists have imported these concepts into the legal realm without adapting them to the specific features of the legal environment (Miceli 1997; Mercuro & Medema 1997; Polinsky 2003; Shavell 2004; Cooter & Ulen 2008;). As a result, law and economics scholarship is predominantly concerned with the *content* of legal rules rather than the *process* by which such rules are created. A legal regime is efficient when no additional gains from trade can be obtained through changes in the allocation of rights; that is, it is efficient when the sum of individuals' surpluses is maximized.[1]

The idea underpinning this idea of efficiency is the "commodification" of legal rights. Namely, if legal entitlements are treated as "commodities" that people (absent transaction costs and wealth effects) can freely buy and sell, then those

This paper was prepared for presentation at The 52nd Annual Meetings of the Public Choice Society, San Antonio, Texas, March 12-15, 2015.
I am grateful to Nuno Garoupa, Giorgio Rampa and Michael Trebilcock for comments on earlier drafts.

[1] Holding constant existing technology, available resources, and individual preferences and setting aside (temporarily) the transaction cost issue.

rights will be allocated, through the process of repeated private bargaining, to their highest-valued use. Crucially, the commodification of legal entitlements is associated with the separation of rights from their formative processes: It is the insulation of the output from the law-making process that enables economists to treat legal entitlements as "commodities."[2] Yet the commodification comes at the price of separating substantive legal rules from the law-making process. This is an inaccurate methodology. While there is no denying that economic theory offers invaluable insights into the analysis of law, it must be recognized that the adoption of mainstream neoclassical economic methodology *without* careful adaptation to the structural peculiarities of the legal environment is not a defensible methodological approach to legal economic analysis.

It is maintained here that legal efficiency is rooted in the process by which members of a community express their consensus and reach an agreement regarding the reallocation of legal rights. Legal efficiency is not an objective property of the outcome independent of the process; rather, it is a function of the ability of the law-making process to embody, in a cost-effective manner, the general consensus of all the people concerned. In this view, legal efficiency becomes a function of the interaction between institutional and environmental variables located at the process level. These variables capture both the institutional features of the law-making process (e.g., the degree of centralization or the ex ante-ex post perspective of law-making) and the characteristics of the regulated environment (e.g., the homogeneity, frequency, and/or complexity of the regulated cases, etc.). Once this logic is recognized, the problem of legal efficiency becomes one of identifying the comparative advantages and disadvantages of alternative sources of law in relation to the characteristics of regulated environments. This entails, of course, a more sophisticated evaluation than that involved in the assessment of specific allocative outcomes. Despite its increased complexity, however, the process efficiency analysis described in this paper provides explanatory and normative tools that usefully complement conventional methodology.

The analysis developed in this paper is certainly not sufficiently mature to be regarded as a systematic "theory" of law-making; nonetheless, it is comprehensive enough to propose a preliminary "framework" upon which a more systematic comparative institutional analysis could be developed in the future.[3] To date, no one in the literature—with a few notable exceptions

[2] This is congenial to economists' prevailing attitude regarding the prediction of efficient *equilibria* resulting from competitive market interactions.

[3] Ostrom (2005) provides a useful distinction between "framework" and "theory". "Frameworks (…) attempt to identify the universal elements that any relevant theory would need to include. (…) The elements contained in a framework help the analyst generate the questions that need to

(Komesar 1994; Parisi & Fon, 2009) [4]–has attempted to propose a general economic theory of law-making; it is likely that the failure to provide such a general theory is due to the lack of a commonly agreed upon unified analytical framework. In this respect, the unified framework proposed here lays the groundwork for a systematic theory of law making.

I proceed as follows. Section I addresses the concept of efficiency as a legal concern. It begins by identifying the structural peculiarities of the legal environment that contradict in many important respects some of the assumptions underlying conventional economic models. These considerations introduce my general contention that an "output bias" underlies conventional law and economics methodology. It is argued that conventional output-oriented methodology is susceptible to the following shortcomings: 1) it is affected by logical circularity and/or logical incompleteness, 2) it fails to provide any assurance of increased social welfare, 3) it does not account for the presence of losers, and 4) it does not account for the predictability/adaptivity trade-off associated with legal change. In these respects, the perspective introduced by a constitutional political economy offers advantages. Section II sketches the outline of a comprehensive theoretical framework designed to predict efficiency problems with the law that incorporate transaction-cost economics within a constitutional political economy. Finally, Section III illustrates the proposed process efficiency analysis more concretely using an example from tort law.

2. EFFICIENCY AS A LEGAL CONCERN

This subsection identifies the structural features of the legal environment that are at odds with the output-oriented perspective. To be clear, it does not object to the unrealistic nature of conventional assumptions used in law and economics models. The sacrifice of realism goes hand-in-hand with the modeling of social

be addressed when first conducting an analysis. (…) Theories enable the analyst to specify which components of a framework are relevant for certain kinds of questions and to make broad working assumptions about these elements. Thus, theories focus on parts of a framework and make specific assumptions that are necessary for the analyst to diagnose a phenomenon, explain its process and predict outcomes."

[4] Komesar (1994) has proposed a comparative analysis of alternative institutions (i.e., politics, courts and markets) that illuminates the limitations of the prevailing scholarship based on single institutional analysis. Komesar's general analytical framework constitutes an important reference point for all those who engage in a comparative institutional of the sources of law. Parisi & Fon (2009) examine "the relative advantages and the respective limits of alternative sources of law." One important set of tools they use to investigate the structure of law-making costs is modern investment theory. From this methodological perspective, they conceptualize the production of legal rules as an economic investment in which the lawmaker sustains present costs in view of future uncertain benefits.

phenomena (Langlois & Csontos, 1983). However, the appropriateness of these assumptions is challenged on the grounds that they leave too much of the phenomenon under investigation out of the analysis. In particular, the failure to capture the implications of the *legal* nature of the object of reallocation (i.e., a "legal right", as opposed to a "thing" or a "commodity") leads to incomplete analysis.

2.1. The "Legal" Environment

The Process-Outcome Relationship. Everything that is qualified as "legal" is the result of a *process* that confers on the thing a legal nature. [5] From an economic standpoint, both the efficiency of the outcome and the structure of the production costs are affected by the characteristics of this law-making process. On the one hand, individuals are willing to give up some degree of outcome efficiency in order to reduce the costs of law-making (Buchanan & Tullock, 1965). On the other hand, in many instances—and for various reasons, some of which will be discussed below—no available law-making institution is able to predictably generate an allocatively efficient outcome. Therefore, if the law-making process is not incorporated into the efficiency calculation, the marginal efficiency analysis of the outcome remains incomplete and, perhaps, misguided (Veljanovski 1980; Komesar, 1994; Parisi 2001, 2004; Parisi & Fon 2009.

Recenlty, Dari-Mattiacci and Deffains (2007) have nicely captured the importance of the process-outcome relationship. Their following statement provides a useful point of reference:

> "we make a distinction between the efficiency of the products of the lawmaking process and the efficiency of the legal process itself in providing a certain, complete and predictable set of rules at the lowest cost for society [...] We suspect that enhancing the study of the legal process will also advance our understanding of the rules thereby produced" .

Furthermore, conventional law and economics generally underestimates the fact that lawmakers' decisional perspective is that of the "average" case. The allocation of legal entitlements is generally made with respect to "classes" of cases, rather than individual cases. The need to consider classes of situations makes it impossible to identify, let alone negotiate for the consent of, everyone affected by a re-allocation of legal rights. Furthermore, the lawmaker must take

---

[5] It is the law-making process that confers a legal nature to legal rights. A chief concern regarding the diverse set of disciplines related to legal theory, to which law and economics belong, is the relationship between the structure of the legal process and the content of legal rules.

into account the uncertainty inherent in the determination of the relevant facts. The lawmaker usually observes only a random sample of the set of non-uniform cases for potential regulation, such that the body of information is significantly constrained. Therefore, the "efficient" rule inevitably produces inefficient outcomes in a number of cases.

Finally, the analytical focus on single, specific scenarios, rather than on sets of non-uniform cases, fails to fully acknowledge the "joint-consumption" interaction among beneficiaries. First, individuals can hardly be excluded from enjoying the benefits of a favorable legal rule. This may cause free-rider problems, resulting in an under-production of efficient law. Second, legal rules may create negative externalities by imposing involuntary redistributions at the expense of those who do not consent to the allocative outcome, thereby failing to meet the Pareto efficiency criterion. (Buchanan & Tullock, 1965). To summarize, the law-making costs, the efficiency-on-average perspective, and the public-good aspect of legal rules structurally characterize the production of law.

Dealing with Losers.[6] The output-oriented perspective aims at freeing efficiency analysis from value judgments. Although distributional concerns have not been neglected entirely (Trebilcock 1975; Quinn & Trebilcock 1982; Kaplow 1986; Trebilcock 2014) mainstream law and economics is based firmly on the assumption that allocative efficiency and distributional equity should be achieved at different functional stages.[7] However, changes in the allocation of legal entitlements usually increase the well-being of some, while simultaneously decreasing the well-being of others. That is, the presence of losers is an essential component of legal change.[8] This poses two methodological problems. First, the assessment of distributional issues entails interpersonal comparisons of utility, which requires value judgments of the sort that conventional economics seeks to avoid. Second, the dislocation effects associated with legal change generate "transition" costs that often impair the attainment of outcome efficiency.

The Economic Value of Legal Predictability. The production of legal rules involves a trade-off between legal predictability and legal change. On one hand, people are willing to sacrifice a certain amount of average outcome efficiency to be able to

[6] I borrow this expression from Trebilcock (2014)

[7] One task involves understanding the initial distribution of normative resources; another task entials showing how to maximize the value of said resources. While the former is a task for philosophers, historians, or legal theorists, the latter is a proper object of the efficiency analysis of law, which ought to be concerned only with *marginal improvements* with respect to presumptive wealth distributions.

[8] Calabresi (1991) maintains that all legal changes must, *ex ante,* entail some losers and that it is necessary to deal with the presence of losers to formulate normative judgments on the efficiency of a legal change.

more easily predict the legal consequences of their behaviors. That is, people gain a high expected benefit from the existence of a *stable* set of legal rules and are often willing to give up optimal allocations in exchange for higher predictability. On the other hand, people demand some degree of adaptation of law to exogenous changes in the social and economic environment. Institutional reforms designed to promote efficiency from an output-oriented perspective do not often take this economic trade-off into account. Instead, they either neglect the benefits expected from more predictable (although sub-optimal) legal regimes or overlook the high rate of technological change that characterizes some regulated environments.

The Problem of Logical Circularity. Allocative efficiency depends on the initial distribution of resources, which depends on the initial allocation of property rights.[9] Therefore, efficiency is not a unique outcome–there are as many efficient outcomes as many possible initial distributions of property rights. This suggests that, in the absence of a nonefficiency-based theory of rights that allows for a normative judgement on the initial distribution of rights, there is no "unequivocal" meaning to comparing any two alternative allocations of rights. Namely, the determination of outcome efficiency rests on antecedent normative judgements concerning the initial distribution of resources that is taken into consideration as the basis for the efficiency assessment (Schmid & Shaffer, 1964; Schmid, 1989; Mercuro & Medema, 1997).

Hence, the problem with efficiency as a normative criterion is that there are too many possible efficient allocations of rights, and that efficiency provides no basis for choosing among them. Allocative efficiency can be defined only upon prior specification of the normative criteria that one adopts to select the distribution of rights that constitute the basis of the efficiency assessment. Similarly, the identification of costs requires a preliminary normative assessment of whose interest counts. As Schmid (2004) put it: "Costs is a function of rights. It is rights that determine whose interests are costs to others. It is these rights that make it possible for one person's interests to become a cost to another". This confirms that any efficiency assessment of rights must rely on a prior nonefficiency-based theory of rights. It is the structure of legal entitlements that determines efficiency, not the converse.[10] The legal-economic discourse is *positional,* rather

[9] Mishan (1967) has demonstrated that since the law influences the distribution of wealth, the optimal allocation of resources ultimately depends on the structure of the legal order.

[10] Mishan (1967) makes the following three points: "(1) [...] the characteristics of an optimal solution are not uniquely specified but depend, in general, on the existing law; (2) [...] the costs incurred in realizing an optimal outcome, and the question therefore of its "feasibility", also depend upon the existing law, and finally; (3) [...] an optimal solution emerging from conflicts of interest is optimal only with respect to an implicit constraint requiring the area in question to be

than merely technical; it rests on antecedent normative premises that are internal to legal-economic discourse.

If the normative assumptions underlying efficiency analyses are not clearly articulated, a serious problem of logical circularity arises that deprives efficiency analysis of any meaningful content (Samuels, 1978; Leff, 1976).

2.2. Defining Efficiency

I assume that the promotion of individuals' welfare is a central concern of law and legal institutions. [11] The foregoing discussion suggests four methodological tasks that a "legal" efficiency criterion should be expected to accomplish. In particular, such a criterion should:

1) assess the desirability of alternative allocations of legal entitlements based on their impacts on the welfare of individuals and relative to the institutional framework (hereinafter, "welfare");

2) deal with distributional concerns by recognizing that the presence of losers is a structural feature of legal change (hereinafter, "dealing with losers");

3) account for the institutional dynamics of legal change and, in particular, for the trade-off between legal predictability and legal adaptivity (hereinafter, "legal change");

4) acknowledge the positional nature of efficiency analyses, thereby avoiding logical circularity (hereinafter, "logical consistency").

As will become clearer shortly, whether or not an efficiency criterion meets the above requirements depends on how the relationships between "outcomes," "processes," and "consensuses" are construed. Consider the following: First, an allocation of resources *is* a distribution of resources; to reallocate means to redistribute.[12] Therefore, any reallocation involves both efficiency and

---

used in common by the groups or persons having conflicting interests. Once separate areas, or separate facilities, are introduced solutions appear that are Pareto superior to the familiar constrained optimal outcomes".

[11] As will become clearer later, the reference to the welfare of the people can be interpreted in two different ways, depending on whether is measured by *intra*personal or *inter*personal comparison of utilities.

[12] Coleman (1985) demonstrates that "in order to overcome market failure it is necessary to integrate considerations of efficiency *and* wealth distribution" and that "the problem of inefficiency (…) requires attending both efficiency and distributive aspects of the problem".

distributional concerns (i.e., "fairness" in the current terminology). Pursuing efficiency by reallocating rights requires addressing *both* efficiency and fairness concerns.

Second, while efficiency is a property of an outcome, fairness speaks to a concern for the process that achieves the outcome. Efficiency is based on individual consent to the outcome, and fairness concerns the way in which those affected by an outcome give their consent to this outcome. Therefore, outcomes and processes as efficiency and fairness are inextricably related to one another, since they are both functions of individual consent. Conventional methodology claims to insulate outcomes from processes and efficiency from fairness. However, this requires artificially separating the "consensus with the outcome" from the "consensus with the process." This latter step—which, for brevity, I dub "efficiency as outcome consent" or simply "outcome consent"—proves problematic in the context of legal economic analyses.

2.3. Efficiency as Outcome Consent

Conventional efficiency criteria are built on the logical relationship between allocative outcomes and individual consent.[13] On the one hand, a rigorous application of the efficiency test in terms of "actual" consensus undermines the practicability of the efficiency assessment. On the other hand, any attempt to reconcile outcome consent with practicability results in impoverishing consent. The structural features of the legal environment (previously identified) further exacerbate these criticisms. This section briefly assesses alternative constructions of outcome consent in light of the criteria identified in the previous subsection.

2.3.1. The Actual Outcome Consent

Generally, the term "efficiency" refers to the concept of Pareto optimality. The Pareto principle embodies the idea that actual consensus allows social decision-making to achieve ethical neutrality.[14] The source of any Pareto improvement is identified through an *intra*personal comparison of utility (Champman, 2005). Namely, the variation of one individual's welfare is assessed against his or her

---

[13] For an excellent discussion of the role played by consent in the normative justification of efficiency, see Coleman (1987).

[14] Cardinal individual utility is abandoned in favor of the use of *ordinal* individual preferences, which facilitates a comparison of individuals' ordering of alternative social states that does not require the assignment of cardinal values to individual preferences. Cirillo (1979) provides a useful reconstruction of Pareto's economic thought, in which he clarifies the importance of the principle of ethical neutrality in the thought of the Italian economist.

own utility function, rather than against other individuals' welfare.[15] Pareto optimality is achieved when no Pareto-superior moves are available, considering all possible alternative allocations.

Consider two individuals: *c* (the consumer) and *p* (the producer), who have utility functions U_c and U_p, which represent respectively the welfare levels of *c* and *p* and which are not objectively measurable by an external observer. In addition, U_c and U_p are functions of a variable x_n, which represents a particular allocation of legal entitlements. Thus, $U_c = U_c(x_n)$ and $U_p = U_p(x_n)$. According to Paretian logic, the move from one allocation of rights x_1 to another allocation x_2 is a "Pareto improvement" if the utility of one individual, say *c*, increases subject to the constraint that the utility of the other individual, *p*, does not diminish. Formally:

$$U_c(x_2) > U_c(x_1) \land U_p(x_2) \geq p(x_1) \quad (1)$$

Pareto optimality is reached at a point x^* where further reallocations that satisfy condition (1) are not possible. At x^* the utility of individual *c* can be increased only by reducing the utility of individual *p*, and the converse. It is worth emphasizing that according to the prevailing interpretation of Pareto optimality (here criticized), at x^* the social welfare is maximized and no Pareto-superior moves can be made.[16]

---

[15] It is as if individuals are assumed to have *lexicographic* preferences with respect to their own personal utilities. That is, individuals are assumed not to compare their own personal utilities with social utility or with other individuals' utilities; rather, if offered several social states, they invariably choose the social state that offers the highest personal utility, *regardless* of how much social utility (or others' utility) is derived from it.

[16] However–as I explain below in the text–Pareto optimality does not assure social-welfare maximization. The notion of "social welfare" rests on the assumption of *inter*personal comparision of individual utility functions, while Pareto efficiency is based on the idea of *intra*personal comparision of utilities. Pareto himself did not interpret his proposed efficiency criterion as one that identifies a unique social optimum. In this respect, Cirillo, (1979) explains that Pareto in developing his notion of efficiency Pareto did not presuppose the existence of a social welfare function. The utilitarian jusitifcation of Pareto efficiency, according to which the Pareto test allows to maximize the sum of individuals' utilities, is therefore highly objectable. On the utilitarian justification of the Pareto principle and a comparison with alternative normative foundations of Pareto efficiency, see Coleman (1980).

Let me now examine whether Pareto efficiency meets the criteria for defining a legal efficiency criteria identified above. The utility possibility frontier depicted in Figure 1 represents the set of Pareto-optimal points for all possible choices of *x*.

Figure 1 Utility Possibilities Frontier

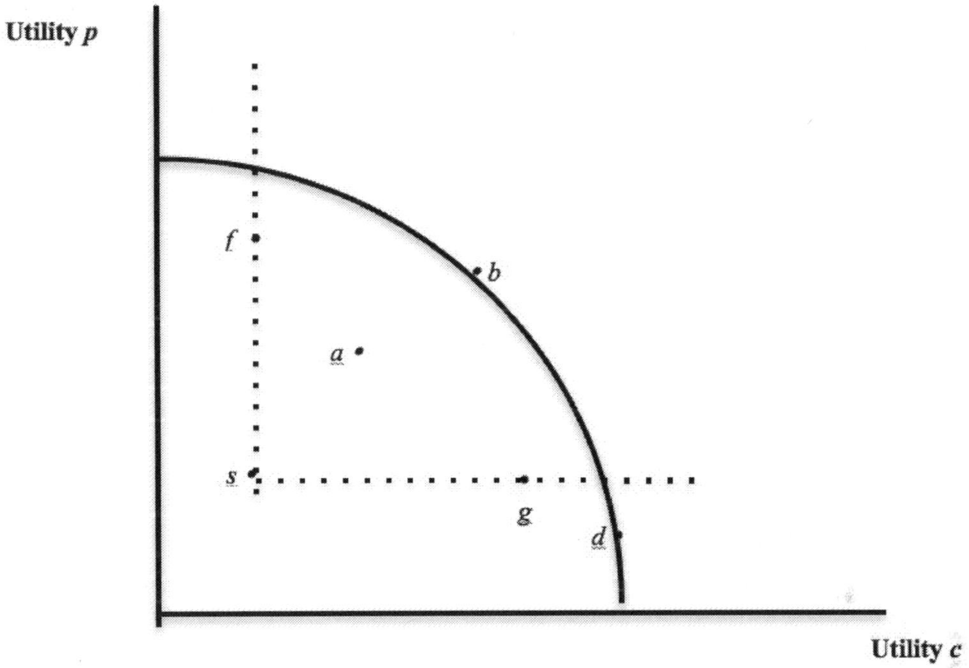

Welfare. First, the *intra*personal comparison of utility does not identify the individual who values a right the most in terms of social welfare. Without measuring the *relative* welfare gains and losses of different individuals, one cannot confidently identify the individual who values the right most highly and whether social welfare has been maximized. Only an *inter*personal comparison of utility (and the related abandonment of Pareto non-cardinality) allows for the identification of the individual who values the contested resource most highly in terms of welfare. Namely, an *intra*personal comparison of utility might well identify a Pareto-superior move that allocates the contested resource to an individual who, according to an *inter*personal evaluation, values the resource *less* (Chapman, 2005). Therefore, while we can say that a Pareto improvement *increases* social welfare (i.e., by increasing at least one person's personal utility), we cannot know with certainty whether it *maximizes* social welfare (i.e., whether the resource has been assigned to the person the values it most highly) (Chapman, 2005).

The preceding considerations can be illustrated by referring to Figure 1. All movements from a point representing the status quo, *s*, to any point located in the north-east region are social-welfare enhancing Pareto improvements–e.g., movements from *s* to *a*, from *s* to *f*, and from *s* to *g*. However, among them Pareto superiority cannot identify which one corresponds to the highest valued use of *x*.[17] Furthermore, we cannot even say that every Pareto-optimal allocation is preferable to non-Pareto-optimal ones from the social-welfare standpoint. For example, *d* is Pareto-optimal but lies outside the north-east Pareto region; therefore, we cannot say that a movement from *s* to *d* improves the welfare of individuals.

Dealing with Losers. First, Pareto optimality does not distinguish between whether optimality is reached through a sequence of Pareto-superior moves or through a different path (i.e., Pareto-inferior moves or non-Pareto-comparable moves).[18] For this reason, Pareto optimality remains blind to the presence of losers on the path to Pareto optimality. For example, a move from *s* to *b* reaches Pareto optimality through a Pareto superior move (i.e., no-losers; in this example, both *p* and *c* win). On the contrary, a reallocation from *s* to *d* reaches Pareto optimality through a non-Pareto-superior move (i.e., *c* wins, *p* loses). Both sequences lead to Pareto optimality, but while the former does not entail losers, the latter make one person better off and the other person worse off.

Hence, Pareto improvements can usually be realized only if compensation is actually paid. That is, when policy issues involve situations with both winners and losers, a unanimous actual outcome consensus can be reached only through full compensation. However, if the costs associated with the compensation mechanism exceed the benefits gained from the Pareto improvement, then the logic of Paretian superiority leads to incorrect results.[19]

---

[17] In *g*, person *c* is better off while *p* is indifferent; by comparison, in *f* person *b* is better off and *c* is indifferent; but, absent any cardinal measure of preference intensity, we cannot say whether *c* or *p* values the right the most. Again, c prefers *g* to *a* (and *d* to *g*); similarly, *p* prefers *b* to *a* and *f* to *b*, but this does not allow a "social" valuation for which a social welfare function is needed.

[18] Coleman (1980) shows that a "Pareto optimal distribution can be reached either by Pareto superior steps or 'moves,' by Pareto inferior moves, or by a combination of the two."

[19] Sen (1970) explains that, depending on the characteristics of the relations between individual preferences, the Pareto notion of efficiency might fail to fulfill the important property of *completeness*. More precisely, the Pareto test fails to provide guidance when individuals have strictly *opposite* preferences.

To summarize, Pareto optimality: 1) cannot compare movement *within* the Pareto frontier; 2) cannot compare movement *along* the Pareto frontier; 3) does not ensure that every allocation *along* the frontier is preferable to every other allocation *within* the frontier. It only ensures that a Pareto-optimal point is preferable to any non-optimal point that is located in the southeast region. In essence, Pareto optimality suffers from incompleteness: It provides no guidance unless there is a unanimous consent among all individuals regarding the preference order with regard to *at least* one couple of alternative states of affairs.

Legal Change. Due to the focus on the allocation of the outputs of the law-making process, Pareto optimality does not allow for comparisons among alternative law-making processes, nor does it allow for a comparative assessment of how such processes differentially affect outcome efficiency. The predictability-adaptivity trade-off is foreign to the analytical scope of Pareto efficiency.

Logical Circularity. Consider the previous example. Assume that the two individuals are confronted with a social choice between two legal states defined by alternative rules of product liability: x_1 is defined by a negligence rule and x_2 is defined by a regime that imposes strict liability upon firms for injuries related to their sold products. c is better off in x_2 and worse off in x_1, while p is better off in x_1 and worse off in x_2. If the *status quo* Q is x_1, then x_1 will be the Pareto-optimal allocation of rights, as it is not possible to move to x_2 without making p worse off. Conversely, if the *status quo* is x_2, then x_2 will be Pareto optimal, as it is not possible to move to x_1 without making c worse off. This shows that, when a legal issue has distributive implications, the *status quo* is regarded as a Pareto-optimal allocation. Namely, Pareto optimality is a function of the initial distribution of rights.

2.3.2 The Hypothetical Compensation Test

Most law and economics scholarship employs the Kaldor-Hicks (hereinafter, "KH") test as the concept of efficiency.[20] KH efficiency embodies the idea that hypothetical compensation is sufficient to achieve a unanimous consensus from members of a society. Compensation is not necessarily paid to the losers; instead, the theoretical *possibility* of compensation is sufficient for the efficiency claim. At first glance, KH efficiency seems to reconcile the Pareto principle (i.e., the idea of efficiency as outcome consensus) with the presence of losers in the reality of policy-making.[21] However, the shift from actual to "hypotethical" compensation

20 This concept of efficiency traces back to the contributions of Kaldor (1939) and Hicks (1941).

21 Bodway & Bruce (1984) provides a useful explanation of the principle of compensation as a theoretical device for separating efficiency and equity.

involves a shift from *intra*personal to *inter*personal comparison of utility that poses more problems than it solves.

Consider the previous example and assume the *status quo* $Q = x_1$. The KH test asks whether c gains enough, in the move from x_1 to x_2, to hypothetically compensate p for her losses and still be better off. Crucially, unlike Pareto effieincy, here *the monetization of the relative gains and losses allows for the inter-personal comparison of utilities.*[22] That is, individuals' utility functions are measured in money terms. Let ω_c and ω_p represent the wealth levels of c and p measured in monetary terms (i.e., how much individuals would pay to have the welfare deriving from a particular allocation of legal entitlements x_n). In addition, let K denote the hypothetical compensation paid by c to p to compensate for her loss of welfare. A change in the allocation of right is regarded as a KH improvement if it satisfies the following condition:

$$U_c(\omega_c(\chi_2) - K) > U_c(\omega_c(\chi_1)) \wedge U_p(\omega_p(\chi_2) + K) \geq U_p\left(\omega_p(\chi_1)\right) \quad (2)$$

Welfare. The major criticism of KH efficiency is that hypothetical compensation (in our example, *K*) ensures neither that the losers' loss of welfare is effectively compensated, nor that the gainers' gain in welfare is effectively larger than the losers' loss.[23] In fact, while actual compensation allows losers to evaluate their losses according to their own welfare functions (thus ensuring that social welfare is not diminished),[24] hypothetical compensation entails that various collective bodies assess relative gains and losses through a hypothetical evaluation based on money sums. With monetized KH test, we lose the assurance that the welfare losses suffered by losers in the reallocation of rights are adequately compensated

[22] Hypothetical compensation requires some measurement of gains and losses. As I will explain below in the text, the monetization of individuals' utility functions is the source of major criticism of KH efficiency test as a legal efficiency criterion.

[23] Champman (2005) demonstrates that "(…) in a Kaldor-Hicks superior re-allocation (…) it is possible that all we have accomplished is the transfer of a good from someone who values it more highly to someone who values it less highly and, therefore, a loss of total welfare overall." Le Grand (1991) also clarifes this point.

[24] Observe that losers would not agree to compensation that does not effectively offset their suffered losses.

by the utility they receive from monetary compensation. [25] This leads to the conclusion that KH efficiency does not accurately identify social welfare improvements.[26]

Dealing with Losers. KH efficiency ignores distributional concerns. All that it is concerned with is the aggregate increase in real income for the whole of society. The fact that gains and losses are measured in terms of *willingness to pay* exacerbates this shortcoming. [27] Since willingness to pay depends on *ability to pay*, KH favors the allocation of resources to wealthier people, who thereby acquire a greater willingness to pay than the poor. This increased willingness to pay will, again, favor the rich in future allocations of resources, thereby causing even further increases in the willingness to pay, and so on.[28]

Legal Change. KH poses an unresolved institutional choice problem: that is, which institutional process is best able to measure gains and losses in the reallocation of resources and to evaluate the plausibility of compensatory measures? On this view, only a comparative institutional analysis is able to identify the conditions necessary to enhance social welfare. When informational and measurement problems do not allow for a sufficiently confident assessment of the relative magnitudes of gains and losses or the plausibility of hypothetical compensation, KH offers no guidance. In addition, when the costs of institutional compensating mechanisms are likely to be greater than the benefits of reallocating resources, KH might lead to incorrect results.

---

25 The reasons can be different. First, the marginal utility of money differs across people depending on their income levels. Second, external factors might determine a utility differential between gainers and losers with respect to the same sum of money. For example, the availability of goods that can effectively replace, in terms of utility, the lost resource might not be sufficient to compensate losers. Third, individuals have different levels of "productivity" in terms of converting the monetary compensation received into actual utility.

26 Champman (2005) clarifies that despite the gainers' gains are larger than the losers' losses in monetary terms, still the monetary value received by gainers might not enable them to generate a utility large enough to offset the losers' losses. Adler (2000) and Mathis (2009) provide a similar critique to KH efficiency.

27 The KH test assumes implicitly a *constant* and *equal* marginal utility for all individuals. As Le Grand (1991) demonstrates, rather than achieving neutrality, KH efficiency conceals a peculiar social welfare function that systematically values rich people more than poor people. Similarly, Markovits (1993) emphasizes that the standard, monetized KH test does not consider that the monetary evaluation of gains and losses is positively wealth elastic.

28 Mathis (2009) observes that, as a consequence of a rigorous application of the KH test, "the rich would get even richer and their ability and willingness to pay would rise continually".

Logical Consistency. As Ellerman (2009) has recently demonstrated, a Numeraire fallacy undermines the logical consistency of KH efficiency.[29] For our purposes, Ellerman's critique is important for two reasons. First, it emphasizes the methodological difficulty of separating distribution and efficiency and the need for antecedent normative specifications in any efficiency analysis. Second, it shows the tautological character of an efficiency analysis when the normative premises underlying the definition of output are not expressly stated.[30]

2.3.3. The Hypothetical Consent Test

The strategy commonly adopted in law and economics to evaluate the desirability of legal doctrines is based on a particular set of methodological assumptions. First, efficiency is characterized as an *objective* property of social states. Second, it is assumed that, in the absence of transaction costs, rational actors will agree to the efficient outcome.[31] Third, it is also assumed that the objective function individuals seek to maximize is aggregate wealth. Based on these assumptions, according to Richard Posner, analysts should assess outcome efficiency by answering "the hypothetical question whether, if transactions costs were zero, the affected parties would have agreed to the institution" (Posner, 1992). That is, law should mimic the outcome of a hypothetical frictionless market, implicitly assuming that individuals in this idealized contest will consent to the wealth-

[29] The Numeraire fallacy is associated with the use of the same numeraire (i.e., money) to measure both efficiency and distribution. Ellerman (2009) observes that, while according to its proponents KH efficiency is based on the separation of *efficiency* and *distribution*, efficiency is assessed through the same numeraire by which distribution is measured. However, if the transfer of resources undertaken to compensate losers is measured with the same numeraire used to measure the "size of the pie," there will never appear to be any increase or decrease in the size of the pie, and any KH move will appear to be a mere re-distribution of resources.

[30] In addition to the Numeraire fallacy that I have emphasized in the text, KH efficiency is subject to a further problem of logical consistency. Scitovsky (1941) demonstrated that in some cases two different states of affairs might be Kaldhor-Hicks efficient to one another. This is generally known as the Scitovsky Paradox. However, it should be noticed that the Scitovsky paradox does not have significant relevance in limiting in practice the use of the KH test in law and economics. In practical terms it occurs when, in the transition from one state to another, a change in income distribution occurs so that the preferences of the winners and the losers differ substantiallyThis occurs for those projects that are of such a scale in relation to the total economy as to bring about strong income effects with consequent relevant changes in prices. Conversely, when the dimension of a project is small relative to the total economy, so that the influence on prices is not significant, it is unlikely that a problem of inconsistency in the result of cost-benefit analysis rises.

[31] That is, it is assumed that consensus follows preferences.

maximizing outcome.[32] From this perspective, the right is allocated to the person who values it the most.[33]

The wealth maximization criterion[34] (hereinafter "WM") asks upon what allocation *c* and *p* would agree in the absence of transaction costs. From this perspective, it is assumed that in the (hypothetical) frictionless world individuals would agree on an aggregate-wealth-maximizing rule: i.e., absent transaction costs, *c* and *p* individuals would agree on the allocation of legal entitlements that maximize their total wealth.

Let W represent the sum of the utilities of *c* and *p*. In keeping with the previous example, the wealth-maximizing allocation of right satisfies the following condition:

$$\max_{x_n} W\big(U_c, U_p\big) = U_c(\omega_c(x_2) - K) \text{ subject to } U_p(\omega_p(x_2) + K) \geq U_p(\omega_p(x_1)$$

(3)

Welfare. By summarizing individuals' preferences into a process of social wealth maximization, this approach eventually eliminates genuine consensus. Efficiency is the maximization of social utility, independent of individual genuine outcome consent. As Coleman (1987) observes, consensus is dissolved into the objective function of aggregate wealth measured in terms of individuals' willingness to pay. There is nothing in the consensus that is not already incorporated into efficiency, as objectively measured through the metric of market prices. In short, this approach ultimately fails to find a consensual, normative justification of efficiency independent from the utilitarian argument (Coleman, 1987).

Dealing with Losers. Like KH efficiency, WM also fails to recognize the distributional effects of legal change, thereby privileging and reinforcing the

---

32 In practice, Posner turns the idea of wealth maximization (hereinafter, "WM") into an "auction rule:" legal entitlements should be conferred on the party who is willing to pay the highest price.

33 Notice that intrapersonal comparison of utility is abandoned. Individual preferences are cardinalized through market prices so to allows for interpersonal comparison of relative gain and losses.

34 Strcitly speaking, WM is not an efficiency criterion. See, on this point, *supra* note 16, Coleman, "Efficiency," 521.

existing wealth distribution. (Bebchuck, 1980). First, because prices reflect a *given* distribution of wealth, measuring preferences by means of market prices (i.e., willingness to pay) involves an assumption that the *status quo* is exogenous to the wealth-maximizing decision (Bebchuck, 1980). Second, WM is based on an external, tacit determination of relevant interests. It does not provide any selective criteria for determining *whose* interests should count in the WM calculus. (Samuels & Mercuro, 1984). From this perspective, it would be better understood in the light of an explicit discussion of the normative assumptions about the relevant interests to be counted as the ultimate objects of WM.

Legal Change. The lack of inquiry into the structure of the law-making process prevents WM from examining the relative merits of alternative sources of law (Komesar, 1994).[35] WM proponents indulge in the methodological error of *inferring the characteristics of the process from the quality of the outcomes.* The observed allocative efficiency of common law rules leads Posner to conclude that the judicial process yields efficient results. Both the positive claim (i.e., that common law is an efficiency-seeking system) and the normative claim (i.e., that common law ought to maximize social wealth) seem to lack sound theoretical foundations (Hadfield, 1992; Garoupa & Gomez, 2011). Without a coherent theory of the law-making process to identify the preferences, incentives and constraints of the actors involved, Posner's positive and normative claims bear the features of ideological assertions, rather than those of warranted theoretical propositions (Mercuro & Ryan, 1984).

Logical Consistency. First, the reliance of WM on the price system involves logical circularity. Because wealth maximization leads to different outcomes depending on assumptions about the initial rights distribution, an antecedent specification of rights is necessary to determine those prices on which wealth maximization relies (Samuels, 1981; Bebchuck, 1980). WM cannot be employed to determine the rights on which it ultimately rests (Coleman, 1980).[36] Second, wealth is an "instrumental" value; it serves as a means to promote other values. The instrumental nature of wealth implies the need to further specify the notion of wealth as the object of maximization (Coleman, 1980).

The analysis to this point suggests that determining efficiency criteria by focusing solely on terminal allocative results leads to unsolved contradictions between a

---

[35] Komesar (1994) elucidates the *single*-institutional nature of conventional law and economics. In paticular, Komesar emphasizes that Posner's economic analysis of law fails to investigate the *relative* advantages and disadvantages of common law over alternative law-making institutions. Thus, Posner's positive claim falls into the Nirvana fallacy.

[36] Coleman (1980) emphasizes that wealth maximization is incapable of generating an initial assignment of rights.

consensual justification of efficiency and the need for normative guidance in real-world policy contexts. It also shows that output oriented criteria do not meet the criteria for a legal efficiency criterion. In particular, 1) they fail to provide any assurance of increased social welfare, 2) they do not account for the presence of losers 3) they do not account for the predictability/adaptivity trade off associated with legal change; 4) they are affected by logical circularity and/or logical incompleteness. The next sub-section introduces the idea that one way to mitigate these contradictions is to extend the Pareto test to the constitutional choice stage.

2.4. Efficiency as Constitutional Consent

The body of scholarship known as "constitutional political economy," which originated in the work of James Buchanan, provides a useful analytical perspective to investigate the efficiency of the law. Although, Buchanan did not develop a framework for a comparative analysis of alternative law-making mechanisms, the methodology he proposed provides useful insights. His methodological strategy (hereinafter referred to as "unanimous constitutional consent") differs from conventional output-oriented methodologies in three important respects. First, Buchanan proposes a *subjective* notion of economic efficiency, according to which unanimous agreement is the only test for efficiency. Anything that is non-unanimously agreed to is inefficient (Buchanan, 1977). Unanimity is regarded as a normatively attractable criterion because it secures the protection of individuals' autonomy and constitutes a means to achieve the enhancement of individuals' welfare.[37] Second, the unanimity test is applied at the constitutional choice stage, which logically precedes the decision regarding the terminal allocative results of the exchange. (Buchanan, 1962). In essence, the idea of enhancing individuals' welfare through Pareto-superior moves is applied at the choice between alternative institutional frameworks (Buchanan, 1962). Third, outcomes that are efficient under one institutional framework cannot be compared with those that are efficient under alternative institutional frameworks. The focus of the efficiency analysis shifts from choices "within" to choices "between" institutional frameworks. Such choices are based on the methodology of hypothetical contractarianism (Buchanan, 1975). In sum, efficiency is the outcome of free and voluntary interactions within specific

[37] While there is no denying that part of the normative attractiveness of unanimity is independent of its impact in terms of efficiency, it is also true that unanimity is attractive for reasons related to efficiency. As Buchanan contends, unanimity is the only test that can ensure that a change is *beneficial* to all the parties affected by a re-distribution. Coleman (1987) proposes a different understanding of Buchanan's idea of efficiency; namely, he maintains that, by adopting unanimity as the only test for efficiency Buchanan reduces entirely efficiency to unanimity.

institutional frameworks. It is a function of the *process* of voluntary exchange and is determined *relative* to a particular framework of exchange.

The focus on the constitutional choice stage enables efficiency analysis to overcome some of the limitations of the output-oriented approach. First, unanimous constitutional consent is not subject to the inability to identify the social-welfare-maximizing allocation of legal entitlements. From a constitutional perspective, the problem of efficiency is not to maximize the objective properties of the outcome, but, rather, to identify the existence of potential gains-from-trade associated with institutional choice. The efficiency of the outcome is not directly measured; rather, it is inferred through the structure of the process from which it is generated. (Buchanan, 1959, 1984). This is the opposite of conventional output-oriented approach that, as noted above, infers consensus from the efficiency of the outcome. Second, the search for unanimous constitutional consent leads legal efficiency analyses to account for (at least to some extent) distributional concerns associated with alternative legal regimes. In fact, the law-making mechanism is the means by which societies deal with the distributional issues associated with making choices among legal regimes. Therefore, the constitutional choice among alternative law-making mechanisms necessarily incorporates distributional concerns. Third, the constitutional choice stage involves a shift of focus from "individuals' incentives as shaped by the law" to "individuals' incentives to produce efficient law." This enables an efficiency analysis to capture the institutional determinants of legal change. An analysis of the incentives faced by those actors involved in law-making facilitates an understanding of how differently alternative law-making mechanisms impact the efficiency of legal change. Finally, it must be recognized that unanimous constitutional consent does not *per se* solve the problem of logical circularity. Efficiency is determined in relation to the institutional framework, which can be, in itself, the object of choice at a preceding logical level Coleman, 1987). However, the methodology of hypothetical contractarianism has the advantage of making explicit the normative premises of the efficiency analysis.

3. Process Efficiency

Having discussed the internal difficulties with the output-oriented approach, I turn now to envisage a complementary methodology based on a systematic focus on the relationship between the efficiency of the law-making process and the the efficiency of the legal output.

3.1. The Consent

Process efficiency analysis builds on the idea of unanimous constitutional consent. It seeks to capture the relationship between the outcome of the law-making process and the law-making process itself by adopting a *constitutional* analytical perspective. Although it focuses on the institutional mechanisms of law creation (i.e., the sources of law), it does not exclude the outcome by the analysis; rather, it assesses the outcome indirectly in light of the analysis of the incentive structure underlying the law-making process. In addition, consistent with the idea of efficiency as constitutional consent, process efficiency analysis does not seek social welfare maximization; instead, it identifies the existence of potential gains-from-trade associated with institutional change.

From a logical standpoint, the focus on the sources of law is consistent with the idea of consensus as an efficiency test. The sources of law are institutional arrangements designed (or emerged) to obviate the fact that unanimity is not achievable in practice at the outcome level. If unanimity could be reached for each final allocative result at no cost, then the spontaneous emergence of law through repeated contractual practice would be the efficient law-making process. Instead, the presence of significant transaction costs associated with creating and enforcing norms explains the emergence in society of institutional "sources of law." Because achieving unanimous outcome consent is costly (due to a variety of factors, some of which I will discuss below), economic actors consent to institutional mechanisms that enable them to save on the costs of unanimity while concurrently legitimizing departures from unanimity. That is, the sources of law are transaction-cost-reducing mechanisms that emerge in response to the cost structure associated with the struggle to achieve the consensus required to legitimize the legal order.

3.2. The Test

Following standard contractarian methodology, I imagine a hypothetical "constitutional convention," in which a group of economic actors who expect to interact repeatedly meet behind a "veil of ignorance" to determine which institutional actor will make the rules to govern their interactions.[38] (Rawls, 1971) This visualization introduces the distinction between the *constitutional* choice stage—in which members of a community choose the mechanisms for producing legal rules (i.e., law-making institutions)—and the *institutional* choice

[38] Harsanyi (1978) develops the idea of a setting in which each actor has the same probability of finding himself or herself in different alternative situations. More recently, Parisi (1995) emphasizes the role of structural, stochastic and induced symmetry in ensuring impersonality of preferences. For a critique of contractarian methodology see Müller, 2002).

stage—in which the lawmaker (under the varying procedural constraints determined at the constitutional level) creates substantive legal rules. Unanimity is required at the constitutional choice stage, which concerns the allocation of law-making powers among alternative law-making institutions (hereinafter, "process-choice"). However, to the extent that unanimous *constitutional* consent is reached, unanimity is not required at the institutional level, which concerns the content of substantive legal rules.

The set of choices includes four alternative and idealized law-making techniques: 1) private legal orderings, 2) adjudication, 3) politics, and 4) agencies and bureaucracies.[39] A source of law is Pareto optimal when no Pareto-superior changes are possible, considering all available alternative law-making mechanisms. Put another way, the optimal law-making mechanism is the one that cannot be modified without the consent of every member of the constitutional convention.

The shift in focus from the outcome of law to the sources of law changes the nature of the efficiency assessment. Individuals that are symmetrically situated at the constitutional choice stage choose institutions by taking into account the relative costs associated with alternative law-making processes and the characteristics of the expected flow of cases to be regulated. So conceived, the efficiency analysis investigates and assesses the *institutional* and *environmental* variables predicted to be most important in affecting the efficiency of legal rules.

3.3. Optimality

The proposed extension of Paretian logic to the allocation of law-making power justifies allocative results that are not efficient, according to the standard, outcome-oriented notion of Pareto optimality. This raises the difficult question of how the Pareto optimality of the process choice is related to the Pareto optimality of substantive legal rules. They relate to each other in various ways, depending on a changing set of institutional and environmental circumstances. However, *it is generally predictable that optimal sources of law tend to generate non-optimal substantive legal rules* due to the presence of high transaction costs associated with the law-making.

I group these costs into three explanatory categories. *Information costs*: Because legal rules are theoretical constructs, the formulation of legal content requires a

39 In practice, the efficient lawmaking process stays with an optimal *mix* of alternative sources of law. The ultimate goal of the process efficiency analysis is to identify the optimal *division of labor* among different lawmaking mechanisms in order to maximize institutional complementarities and comparative advantages.

great deal of knowledge, competence, and experience. The actors involved in the production of law face, therefore, significant information gathering costs. *Agency costs*: The incentives of the lawmaker often diverge from those of the people subject to the law; this undermines the law-making process's degree of responsiveness to the interests and preferences of the people subject to the law. In addition, the latter face considerable difficulties in monitoring the activities of the former, which creates opportunities for lawmakers to create legal rules that serve their own interests. *Adaption costs*: The law-making process faces a difficult trade-off between the costs of (long-run) legal certainty and the costs of changing the law in response to changes in the regulated environments.

In sum, the capacity of legal rules to promote efficiency is constrained by the limited information available to the lawmaker, the misalignment of incentives between the law-maker and the people subject to the law, and the trade-off between legal certainty and efficient legal change. The goal of the law-making process is to minimize the impact of law-making transaction costs on the efficiency quality of legal rules, thereby achieving what I call, respectively, "technical efficiency," "agency efficiency," and "adaptive efficiency." In my proposed terminology, these are the three components of process efficiency analysis.

Once the entire set of law-making costs is included in the efficiency calculus, the closest approximation of the Pareto frontier is generally achieved at a point that cannot be qualified as Pareto-optimal in the standard sense. Because, as noted above, Pareto efficiency does not discern among alternative sub-optimal outcomes, an alternative efficiency criterion is needed. I contend that extending the basis of the Pareto test to the outcome-process relationship is one possible way to compare movements (within the Pareto frontier) that are non-comparable on the basis of an actual outcome consensus. The intuition is the following. Because the distance of final allocative results from the Pareto frontier is a function of law-making costs, the ability to assess the relative costs of alternative sources of law facilitates a comparison of the sub-optimal allocations attained by law-making processes. That is, sub-optimal points that are non-comparable under "standard" Pareto efficiency become comparable under process efficiency. However, this is more easily said than done. This section proposes one possible way to conduct a process efficiency analysis.

The idea of comparing sub-optimal points through an assessment of the *relative* magnitudes of the law-making costs associated with alternative sources of law is consistent with the idea of consensus as the basis for the efficiency test. Consent relates to the "process-outcome relationship." Individuals choose the best possible process-outcome ratio—that is, the one that most enhances their welfare, under the constraints of others' preferences and the *status quo*. The attained outcomes are not "optimal" in a standard Paretian sense, but are "optimally" produced. *The lawmaking process is optimal (or "efficient") if there is no other alternative institution that does better, across the circumstances in which it actually operates, in producing legal rules such that each member of society is enabled to enhance his or her own welfare.*

3.4. The Costs: A Taxonomy

The efficiency assessment proposed here requires the identification of a unified taxonomy of law-making costs, which will enable the measurement of the various components of process efficiency across different law-making institutions. The proposed taxonomy organizes the fundamental stages of analysis in assessing the relative merits of alternative law-making processes on a case-by-case basis. It does so by identifying the mechanisms that generate inefficiencies in the production of law. The efficiency of the output is still relevant, but is interpreted as a function of the law-making costs.

Importantly, the complexity of the interplay between law-making costs and the regulated environments does not allow for an identification of a unique cost-minimizing point. Cost functions depend on a large number of variables, whose saliences vary across institutions and situations.

My proposed taxonomy of law-making costs is organized around the three following principles:

1) Law-making costs are grouped into three categories, consistent with the definition of process efficiency: information costs, agency costs, and adaptation costs.

2) Each category has both a "process" and an "outcome" dimension. That is, while some costs are associated with the process of making the law, others are related to the inefficiency of the resulting outcome.[40]

3) Analysis of the variables affecting the law-making costs is organized along the lines of a supply and demand model. The supply side summarizes the features of the law-making process that are predicted to predominantly affect the structure of the law-making costs (i.e., the institutional variables). The demand side summarizes the features of the situation from which the need for law arises in

---

[40] As the discussion proceeds, it will become clear that I categorize outcome inefficiency costs as "law-making" costs because they are a function of the incentives embedded in the institutional structure of the law-making process. That is, they are causally related to the structure of the law-making process.

society (i.e., the environmental variables); it includes both the exogenous conditions of the regulated environments and the preferences, incentives, and constraints of the people subject to the law.

Information Costs. The law-making information costs include 1) information-gathering costs, 2) compliance information costs, and 3) participation information costs. First, the lawmaker bears information costs to develop the content of legal rules and assign legal entitlements. I call these costs "production-information costs." Second, people who are subject to the law bear costs related to becoming informed about the content of legal rules. I call these costs "compliance information costs." Third, the participation of the relevant actors in the law-making process requires the gathering of significant amounts of information.[41] I call these costs associated with participation in the law-making process "participation information costs."

Agency Costs. Agency costs measure the degree of responsiveness of the law-making process to the interests of the individuals subject to the law. From this standpoint, the analysis focuses on the principal-agent relationship between the people (i.e., the beneficiaries of legal rules) and the lawmaker, to whom people delegate the law-making power. Generally, differences in incentives between the people subject to the law and the lawmaker, as well as difficulties confronted by the former in observing the behavior of the latter, create room for severe agency problems. It is useful to distinguish among the following categories of agency costs: 1) influence agency costs (or external pressure costs), 2) internal pressure costs, 3) outcome agency costs, and 4) costs of reducing agency costs.

First, "influence agency costs" are generated by incentive misalignment among different groups of principals: that is, rent-seeking competition among various pressure groups that leads to the dissipation of resources that could be more productively employed elsewhere. This resource dissipation is usually referred to in the literature as "rent-seeking costs." Second, "internal pressure costs" are associated with the lawmaker's moral hazards (i.e., the lawmaker's opportunistic behavior, which often occurs to the detriment of the principals' interests). These manifest in various forms. Consider, for example, the rent-extortion costs (McChesney, 1987, 1997) and transaction-augmented costs (Twight, 1994) in the

[41] For example, in the political process, voters bear significant information costs in order to participate in the election of their representatives; in the judicial process, litigants spend a significant amount of resources in collecting and elaborating on the information essential to the adversarial process; and, finally, individuals in the market process bear information costs related to acquiring the information necessary to engage in market transactions (i.e., information on the quality of economic goods, the reliability of the counterpart to the transaction, and so forth).

political process, or the costs of bureaucratic drift in administrative processes.[42] Third, "outcome-agency costs" are associated with successful rent-seeking.[43] These are costs imposed on people subject to the law by inefficient legal rules that result from the opportunistic behavior of lawmakers combined with rent-seeking by pressure groups. These costs manifest themselves in various forms, such as through monopolistic rent costs in the political process or through agency slack on the part of bureaucrats in technocratic law-making. Finally, agency costs are also those associated with the functioning of institutional arrangements designed to minimize the agency problem (i.e., the "costs of reducing agency costs"). Consider, for example, the costs associated with institutional arrangements designed to minimize lawmakers' moral hazards in bureaucratic processes (i.e., the costs associated with *ex ante* and *ex post* control of bureaucratic action by politicians), or the costs associated with instituional arrangments designed to discourage rent-seeking (e.g., the division of powers, a bicameral legislature, etc.).

Adaptation costs. Adaptation costs include: 1) adaption transaction costs; 2) adjustment costs; 3) resistance costs; 4) maladaptation costs. Adaptation transaction costs are those incurred by individuals seeking to appreciate the efficiency advantages of a superior legal regime and to coordinate a simultaneous, mutually advantageous migration towards the new legal regime. Consider, for example, the costs involved, for members of all groups, in appreciating the advantages of a new social norm or in adopting a new technology. First, adjustment costs are those that individuals bear when transitioning to the new legal regime and changing their behaviors as required by the law. These are conduct costs in nature; that is, they are related to the behavioral changes imposed on individuals by the legal change. Third, resistance costs include the cost increments borne by individuals in order to maintain old behaviors. Legal change is often associated with resistance from those individuals who suffer losses due to the new legal rules (i.e., the losers) (Trebilcock, 2014). Resistance also comes from those individuals who are slow to appreciate the advantages of legal change.[44] In general, an individual chooses to adjust to a new legal regime to the point at which the present value of an increment in the adjustment costs equals the present value of an additional increment in resistance costs. Fourth,

---

[42] Influence agency costs and internal pressure costs differ with respect to the source of the rent-seeking activity. While internal pressures derive from rent-seeking efforts on the part of officials operating within the law-making arena, external pressures derive from various stakeholders' efforts to extract rents from the law-making process.

[43] Influence agency costs and internal pressure costs are independent of whether the rent-seeking efforts of agents and principals succeed.

[44] Both losers and individuals who do not appreciate the efficiency advantages of legal change tend to stick to "old" norms, thereby incurring resistance costs.

adaptive efficiency has an important outcome dimension. That is, the inefficient adaptation of the production of law to exogenous changes in the demand for law generates substantively inefficient norms.[45] I refer to the costs generated by those substantively inefficient legal rules resulting from the inefficient adaptation of law-making to changes in the demand for law as maladaptation costs. Finally, the levels of information and agency costs identified above have obvious dynamic implications: The higher the agency and information costs are, the slower and less effective the legal change will be. Figure 2 summarizes the discussion.

[45] In the event of a change in the regulatory environment, legal rules that were previously efficient may become inefficient. The mismatch between the supervening inefficient rule and the changing context determines the magnitude of the maladaptation costs.

Figure 2 Unified Taxonomy of Law-making Costs

	Supply Side	Demand Side	Outcome
Information Costs	**(1) Information Gathering Costs** (e.g., costs associated with appreciating people's preferences and estimating the distribution of prospective cases with respect to the variables relevant for regulation)	**(2) Compliance Information Costs** (e.g., costs associated with appreciating the content of legal rules) **(3) Participation-Information Costs** (e.g., costs associated with litigation, with participation in the electoral process, and so on)	**(4) Maladaptation Costs** (e.g., costs associated with the inability of the lawmaker to meet the heterogeneity of local preferences)
Agency Costs	**(1) Internal Pressure Costs** (e.g., rent-extortion costs, augmented transaction costs) **(2) Costs of Reducing the Agency Costs** (e.g., costs associated with checks and balances in the political process, *ex ante* and *ex post* control costs in the bureaucratic process, and so on)	**(3) External Pressure Costs** (e.g., rent-seeking costs)	**(4) Outcome Agency Costs** (e.g., monopolistic rent costs in the political process or bureaucratic and legislative drift in the bureaucratic process)
Adaptive Costs	**(1) Dynamic Implications of Information and Agency Costs**	**(2) Adaptation Transaction Costs** (e.g., the cost of appreciating the advantages of legal change) **(3) Adjustment Costs** (e.g., costs of adopting new behavioral standards) **(4) Resistance Costs** (e.g., costs of maintaining old behaviors)	**(5) Maladaptation Costs** (e.g., costs of legal obsolescence, or retardations in adaptations to changes in the regulated environment)

3.5. The Supply of and Demand for Law

The final step in the process efficiency analysis is to identify those variables that are predicted to be most important in affecting the structure of the law-making costs (and, thereby, of determining the relative efficiency of alternative sources of law). In this respect, it is useful to organize the inquiry along the lines of a supply of and demand for law. As has been repeatedly emphasized, the central hypothesis is that *the efficiency of law depends upon the interplay between the demand for and supply of law*—that is, the interaction between institutional and structural variables that is at work within the formation process of law determines the efficiency properties of the outcome. Figure 3 illustrates the analytical framework of the process-outcome relationship.

Figure 3. The Process-Outcome Relationship

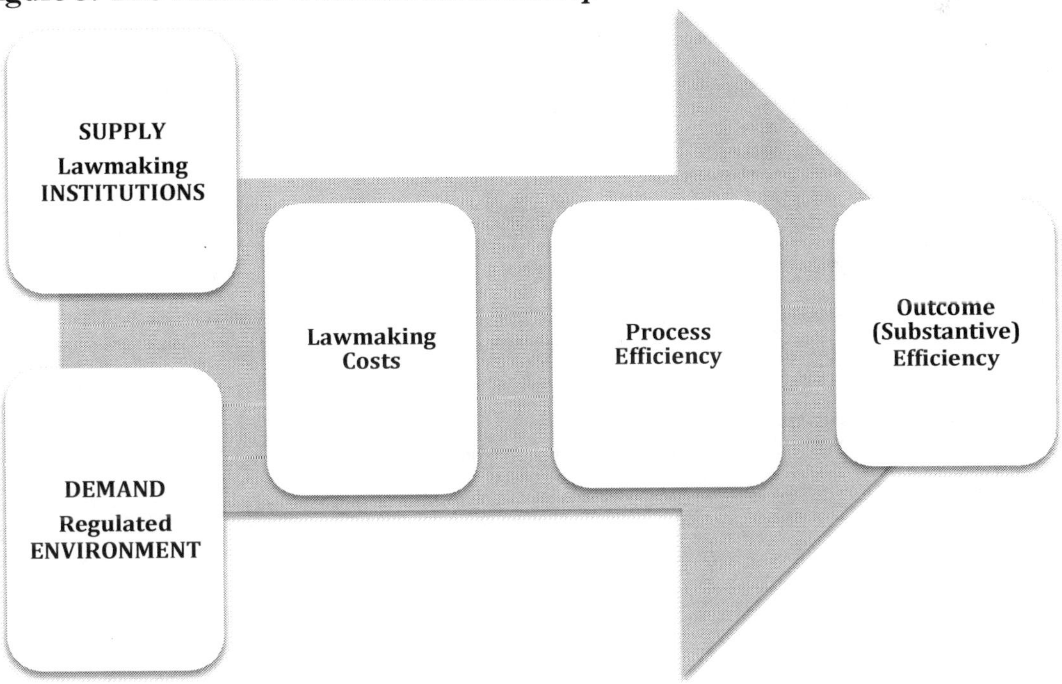

Let me succinctly provide some explanatory examples of variables affecting law-making costs. It is convenient to proceed at two levels of abstraction. At the highest level of abstraction, it is possible to identify four variables (two institutional and two structural) that most affect law-making costs. On the supply side, the *ex ante* versus *ex post* dimensions and the degree of centralization of law-making significantly affect the three components of process efficiency.[46] On the demand side, the degrees of *frequency* and *homogeneity* of the behaviors subjected to regulation largely determine the optimal mix of *ex ante* and *ex post* regulation and of *centralized* versus *decentralized* law-making.[47]

This four-dimensional framework of law-making allows for the formulation of three general hypotheses, to be tested against the results of the comparative institutional analysis on a case-by-case basis. First, under conditions of high homogeneity and frequency of the demand for law, the *ex ante* centralization of law-making allows for significant economies of scale, which significantly reduce the average (production and compliance) information costs. Second, *ex ante* centralization entails a significant increase in the agency costs of law-making. Third, *ex ante* centralization reduces the magnitude of the adaptation transaction costs associated with legal change. It increases the magnitude of resistance and maladaptation costs when the legal demand is heterogeneous and when both the aggregate frequency and the frequency *per actor* increase.

At the lower level of abstraction, additional institutional and environmental features, which vary across institutions, might exacerbate or counterbalance the effects of *ex ante* versus *ex post* and of centralized versus decentralized dimensions. Let me provide some examples.

Information Costs. In politics and bureaucracy, the information advantages of ex ante centralization must be weighed against the disadvantages associated with the high irrationality and limited information capabilities of the political law-maker and the tendency toward overregulation and output ineffectiveness of the bureaucratic processes. Adjudication enjoys comparative advantages in that it allows for greater responsiveness of the production of law to local preferences in a context characterized by high heterogeneity. Private law-making produces

---

[46] *Ex ante* law-making produces legal principles that are applicable to classes of cases included within the scope of the law. This entails that, from an economic perspective, the fixed costs of creating legal principles are borne only once.

[47] On one hand, the *frequency* of the regulated behavior affects the variable component of the cost function, and the high level of frequency enables the lawmaker to distribute the high fixed costs of ex ante law-making over a high number of legal cases. On the other hand, the homogeneity of legal demand (i.e., when the elements that determine the need for legal intervention occur in *similar* fashions) enables the lawmaker to organize the application of a *single* legal response to an indefinite number of facts of law. Namely, if a sequence of potential cases that gives rise to a specific economic need are similar with regard to how they can be addressed by the law, then the lawmaker can shape the same institutional legal response to all cases. From this perspective, the homogeneity increases the *marginal productivity* of the *ex ante* law-making. Furthermore, the *homogeneity* of the legal demand allows for the regulation of prospective legal cases with a high level of *ex ante* legal precision.

efficient legal rules only under the very restrictive conditions of close-knittedness (Ellickson, 1991; Bernstein, 1992; Cooter, 1992).

Agency Costs. In politics, three institutional features *exacerbate* the agency costs associated with *ex ante* law-making: the rational ignorance of the electorate as a whole, the majoritarian character of political decision-making, and the collectivized nature of the legislative outcome. Administrative law-making entails bureaucratic drift costs, as well as costs related to the strategic use of delegation by politicians, which exacerbate the agency problem associated with *ex ante* centralization. In adjudication, the doctrine of *stare decisis* accentuates the *ex ante* dimension of judicial law-making, thereby further increasing the rent-seeking pressures aimed at influencing the evolution of precedents. Private law-making significantly decreases agency costs (although it is not immune from the agency problem). However, even in the context of private legal orderings, as the degree of centralization increases and the law-making adopts an *ex ante* perspective (e.g., industry "self-regulation"), agency costs increase significantly.

Adaptation Costs. The political representative mechanism exacerbates the tendency of *ex ante* centralization to increase resistance and maladaptation costs. This is due to many factors, including: the increasing number of veto players that, in the political process, might block efficient transitions; the increasing number of rent-seeking groups that have incentives to promote inefficient transitions; and the transitional gain trap that prevents efficient legal change (Tullock, 1975). At the same time, however, it must be recognized that the offsetting capabilities of legislators can reduce resistance costs. The *adjudication* process has relative advantages over politics for three reasons: the leveling-of-the-playing-field effect associated with the judicial process; the incremental nature of judicial legal change; and the lower access costs than in the political process. Private legal orderings enjoy comparative advantages in these environments, in which group members are receptive to new technical information and are able to cheaply communicate with one another and coordinate a collective move toward efficient legal regimes. When these conditions are absent, pure, decentralized law-making is subject to the risk of being impeded by evolutionary traps and manipulated by interest groups; hence, it evolves toward or may stabilize the emergence of inefficient legal rules.

4. AN EXAMPLE: PRODUCT SAFETY

This section discusses the issue of product safety. The aim is not to provide a comprehensive discussion, but to provide some examples of how the process efficiency analysis helps to provide a different understanding of legal-economic issues that complements the traditional output-oriented perspective.

4.1. Output-Oriented Analysis

Most law and economics scholarship on product safety focuses on the following three issues. First, much discussion focuses on the choice between alternative liability rules (e.g., strict liability versus the negligence rule ("*issue 1*") (Shavell, 1980; Miceli, 1997; Shavell, 2004; Cooter & Ulen, 2008).[48] Second, divergent views have emerged over the issue of whether allowing manufacturers and consumers to design their own liability schemes, through contract, will allow them to shift product-related risks to those who can bear them at a lower cost, thereby enhancing social welfare ("*issue 2*").[49] Third, a stream of scholarship inquires into the choice between tort liability and safety regulation ("*issue 3*"). In this latter respect, there has been a tendency to agree on the complementariness of ex post liability and ex ante regulation, as well as on the social-welfare enhancing effect of the joint use of the two instruments (Shavell, 1984; Kolstad, Ulen, & Johnson, 1990; Schmitz, 2000).[50]

Conventional law and economics approaches each of these issues from an output-oriented, single-institutional perspective. The analysis of *issue 1* focuses on the impact of differing liability rules on the incentives to adopt efficient levels of precaution and engage in the optimal level of risky activities (Shavell, 1980).[51] The source of transaction costs is exogenous to the model, and variations of these costs are independent of the choice between alternative institutional processes and environmental variables. The debate regarding *issue 2* focuses on measuring the imperfections of private markets against an idealized, but unattainable, adjudication process (Bertrand, 2014), thereby exposing the analysis to a Nirvana fallacy. Similarly, the debate on *issue 3* assumes alternative classes of rules (e.g., strict liability, uniform safety standards) to be exogenously given. It investigates the impacts of these outcomes on the incentives structure confronted by potential injurers and injured parties. There is no inquiry into how differentially alternative sources of law affect the content of the outcome.[52]

---

48 According to traditional law and economics prescription, when the technology of precaution is *bilateral*, then the *negligence* standard provides efficient incentives; conversely, when the technology of precaution is *unilateral, strict* liability is considered to be more efficient.

49 Cfr., for example, in favor of a contractual liability regime, Priest (1982, 1991) Schwartz (1992) Ausness (2000). *Contra*, Arlen (2010) Goldberg & Zipursky (2010) Choi & Spier (2013).

50 For a more elaborated position see the recent contribution by Miceli, Rabon, & Segerson, (2013).

51 This approach is dominant in most used law and economics text-books (Miceli, 1997; Shavell, 2004; Cooter & Ulen, 2008).

52 Generally, it is implicitly assumed that the source of "legal liability" is judicial in nature. Little attention is devoted to other institutional sources of legal liability (e.g., statutory or administrative liability). In addition, law-making costs are usually lumped into the sweeping concept of

I do not want to be interpreted as claiming that these analyses are incorrect. However, I suggest that the output-oriented approach needs to be integrated with a complementary analysis of the process-outcome relationship.

4.2. Process Efficiency Analysis

In the following pages, I analyze each of the three components of process efficiency analysis: information, agency, and adaptive efficiency. From this perspective, I show that: *issue 1* is better understood in light of the impact on the law-making costs and in relationship with the overall organization of the sources of law; *issue 2* is misplaced; *issue 3* gains central importance, but from the contrasting perspective of the impact of the ex ante – ex post perspective on the structure of the law-making costs.

Each of the following subsections is organized into two steps. First, it discusses the choice between strict liability and negligence in the area of product safety (*issue 1*). Second, it emphasizes the relative advantages and disadvantages of politics, bureaucracy, judge-made law, and private legal orderings (thereby illuminating *issues 2 and 3*).

4.2.1. Information Efficiency

Strict Liability versus Negligence. One theory that explains the regime of strict liability in the area of product safety is the structure of production information costs. Strict liability increases the degree of centralization in the law-making process and implants an *ex ante* perspective into the context of adjudication (hereinafter, "*ex ante* centralization"). Liability is established prospectively for an entire "class" of cases, regardless of the level of precaution adopted by the injurer. As Epstein (1988) observes, strict liability "reserve[s] to the courts a legal monopoly to fashion the relevant terms and conditions on which *all* products should be sold in all relevant markets."

Process efficiency analysis suggests that, when the demand for safety products is characterized by a high degree of frequency and homogeneity, *ex ante* centralization allows for significant economies of scale with respect to production information costs. From this perspective, the adoption of a regime of strict liability is justified in cases in which the demand for product safety is highly homogeneous and frequent. The traditional class of widely sold products with

administrative costs, summarized into constant variables used in formal models. Finally, the errors of judges are considered in a number of models,[52] as is the uncertainty in the definition of legal standards. However, again, these important variables are not treated as functions of the institutional law-making framework.

manufacturing defects (e.g., exploding Coke bottles) provides a good example of homogeneity and frequency that justifies (from an information efficiency standpoint) a strict liability regime. Far less homogeneous is the stream of designing and warning cases, which is characterized by a higher heterogeneity that causes the marginal informational costs to *vary* from case to case (i.e., are not diminishing), thereby preventing scale effects via the impact on the lawmaking average cost function.

A second reason that explains the regime of strict liability is related to the structure of compliance information costs. Assuming high frequency and homogeneity, if the application of the law is concentrated on a relatively limited number of people—such that the frequency *per actor* is high[53]—strict liability will be combined with a high level of ex ante specificity of the content of legal rules. The reason for this is that higher frequencies *per actor* entail higher expected benefits from compliance—and, thus, higher demand for ex ante law-making, and higher legal specificity on the part of those most frequently subject to the rules. Differently stated, the higher the expected net benefit value from compliance, the greater the amount of resources that the individual is willing to use to increase his or her knowledge of the law. In this respect, observe that the demand for product safety often emerges from economic sectors with sharp polarizations between consumers and producers. That is, a relatively small number of potential injurers (cheaper precaution-takers) are exposed to high frequencies per actor so that the application of the law concentrates upon a relatively limited number of economic actors. In such cases, the regime of strict liability has an advantage in terms of information efficiency, as it enhances the deterrence effect of total liability while reducing the average costs of defining the terms of liability.

The two preceding arguments are consistent with the actual trend among several jurisdictions to adopt strict liability regimes in the area of product safety. The European Union Directive on product safety[54] offers a good example of centralized regulation of product safety. Furthermore, empirical observation shows that many strict liability regimes are *statutory* in nature, which confirms the argument that strict liability is efficient under the same efficiency conditions as *ex ante* centralized law-making.

53 Frequency *per actor* affects the intensity of the behavioural effect by influencing individual incentives to comply with the law. Thus, holding the aggregate frequency constant, when the regulated behaviour is *concentrated* on a few actors, the *high* frequency *per actor* reinforces the behavioural effect. On the contrary, when regulated behaviours are widely *distributed* among the individuals subject to the law, the frequency *per actor* is low, thereby weakening the incentive to comply.

54 Directive 2001/95/EC of 3 December 2001 on General Product Safety

Sources of Law. The last consideration raises the issue of the impact of alternative sources on the definition of the optimal standard of care. This problem is acute when it comes to *risky* products. In fact, this area is often characterized by pervasive outcome uncertainty and requires both specialized competence and technical information on the part of the law-maker (Fraiberg & Trebilock, 1997).

The judicial law-making process proves highly inefficient in defining the content of a tort liability regime in the area of risky products. The *ex post* perspective exposes judicial law-making to cognitive biases in the measurement and assessment of risk. Loss aversion, hindsight bias, anchoring, framing effects, and other cognitive distortions prevent judicial decision-making from identifying efficient safety incentives in the area of risky products. (Rachlinski, 1998) (Guthrie, Rachlinski, & Wistrich, 2001). These inefficiencies are exacerbated by juries' aversion toward corporate risk analysis. Empirical studies have shown that jurors tend to punish those corporations that carry out a cost-benefit analysis, interpreting the higher level of information about risk as an indicator of the intention to inflict the risk (rather than as a sign of corporate responsibility or an effort to achieve risk-cost balancing) (Moore & Viscusi, 1991; Viscusi, 2000).

Economic theory suggests that, because agencies and bureaucracies possess greater cognitive resources (and gather technical information at lower costs) than legislatures, the expected benefit of delegating law-making power to them increases with the complexity and uncertainty of the decision-making (Mitnick, 1980; Aranson et al., 1982). Despite this advantage, the structural features of the bureaucratic process are often at odds with information efficiency (and the efficient allocation of risks). First, when uncertainties emerge from regulatory processes, agencies' regulatory responses to the demand for risk regulation are plagued by the "vicious circle" including public risk perception and congressional action and reaction. (Breyer, 2009). Namely, the bias in the public's perception of risk is magnified by uncertainties regarding the regulatory process, and the increased pressure on agencies is likely to be reflected in a decision-making process that is in various way biased.[55]

Second, because excessive risk-taking, in the context of bureaucratic decisions, is more easily detectable than insufficient risk-taking, bureaucrats tend to over-

[55] Breyer suggests that regulatory inefficiency –manifests in three serious biases. First, agencies exhibit a tendency to focus narrowly on their regulatory mission at the expense of other policy goals (i.e., "*tunnel vision*"). Second, agencies do not prioritize the most significant problems; rather their regulatory priorities are influenced by public misperceptions of risks. (i.e., "*random agenda selection*"). Third, agencies may possess overlapping jurisdictions for the same regulatory issue, which creates the risk of inconsistent regulation when bureaucratic objectives and preferences are not aligned.

estimate the risk of imposing, through regulation, an "excess risk" on society—in comparison to that of allocating "insufficient risk." Said differently, administrative regulation is systematically biased in favor of avoiding Type II errors (i.e., excessive risk), rather than Type I errors (i.e., sub-optimal risk) (Stearns & Todd, 2009), despite the fact that the costs of the latter might be equal to or even greater than those of the former.[56] Third, the institutional insulation from people subject to the law deprives bureaucratic law-making of feedback signals concerning the relative benefits and costs of regulation.[57] In conclusion, during assessments of the information efficiency of law-making through agencies, the advantages of specialized knowledge should be weighed against the costs of bureaucratic insulation.

Private legal orderings enjoy relative advantages in environments characterized by technical *complexity,* in which the identification of standards of conduct requires specialized knowledge on the part of the same economic actors involved in the risky activity. In general, private legal orderings are characterized by the fact that norm producers coincide with both targeted actors and norm-beneficiaries. This increases information efficiency because, unlike centralized law-making bodies, norm producers have a *direct* perception of their costs and benefits. Second, the fact that norm producers and norm beneficiaries are two identical sets of individuals raises the cost of irrational behavior in the process of norm creation—and, thereby, creates incentives to adopt *rational* beliefs and behave accordingly. This is a significant difference from the incentive structure confronted by norm producers in political and administrative processes. The comparative informational advantage of private ordering over other sources of law is consistent with the fact that, in the U.S., the vast majority of the technical standards necessary to protect public safety are developed by private, non-profit organizations. Namely, in crafting public rules, agencies rely on privately created standards by using the practice of "incorporation by reference (Bremer, 2013).

As will be clear shortly, the information advantages of private orderings must be weighed against their disadvantages in terms of adaptive efficiency. However, it is generally recognized in the law and economic literature that the seller-customer

[56] The effect of bureaucrats' risk aversion on the level of regulation can be usefully explained through the concepts of Type I and Type II errors. Type I errors occur when bureaucrats reach the conclusion that *a safe activity is risky*; conversely, Type II errors occur when bureaucrats reach the conclusion that *a risky activity is safe.* In many cases, Type II errors involve more easily detectable societal costs because they manifest in tangible harm to people; on the contrary, Type I errors engender social costs detectable only through a counterfactual assessment of foregone benefits that could have been derived from the safe activity that was not pursued.

[57] Unlike legislators, bureaucrats do not face direct electoral constraints, and, unlike judges, they are not involved in the litigation process between interested parties.

relationship between firms and consumers provides firms with incentives to regulate risk and to subject themselves to liability rules as a signal to consumers of the quality of their products (Daughety & Reinganum, 1995).

4.2.2. Agency Efficiency

This subsection is organized around two steps. First, it explains that the liability regime affects the degree of centralization of the law-making process. Centralization, in turn, increases the expected return from rent-seeking—thereby increasing the external pressures on the law-making body (Patchel, 1993; Ribstein & Kobayashi, 1996). Second, I briefly emphasize the relative advantages and disadvantages of politics, bureaucracy, judge-made law and private legal orderings.

Strict Liability versus Negligence. Compared to negligence, strict liability accentuates the centralization of the supply of law,[58] thereby reducing the costs of coordinating interest group pressures. Consider two opposing scenarios. Under a negligence rule in a decentralized adjudication system, interest groups must engage in rent-seeking activities in each local jurisdiction to obtain favorable decisions. Taken to the extreme, in an ideal, polycentric, decentralized system (with a competitive pluralism of adjudicating bodies), the favorable decision produces effects among the parties to the dispute. Only the parties to a dispute have an incentive to invest in influence activities. Conversely, under a regime of strict liability, in the context of centralized adjudication, the greater uniformity of the law will ensure the uniform application and enforcement of the law across all local jurisdictions. This has three consequences. First, centralization allows rent-seekers to exert pressure at lower cost and greater effectiveness, thus allowing them to exploit economies of scale in rent-seeking (Redoano, 2010). Second, as the degree of centralization increases, it becomes more costly for individuals to opt out of inefficient laws;[59] those individuals who suffer from higher costs from inefficient laws are forced to engage in a relatively more costly "voice" strategy.[60] Third, as a consequence of this effect, centralization involves "outcome" agency costs. Interest group theory has long demonstrated that large, broadly based interests suffer from the problem of collective action, whereas concentrated

---

58 However, also negligence standards can be centralized. For this reason, as emphasized shortly, the characterisitcs of instituional sources of liability rules needs to be anlyzed in relationship with substantive legal rules determining the liability regime.

59 For an excellent discussion of the relationship between exit options and the efficiency of the law, see O'Hara & Ribstein (2000).

60 In contrast, decentralization and inter-jurisdictional competition facilitate the exercise of the exit option, reduce the monopolistic power of the centralized lawmaker, and ultimately limit the returns expected from rent-seeking behaviour.

special interests tend to be advanced more effectively by smaller and more organized interest groups that will manipulate legal outcomes to their advantage (often at the costs of larger, more disorganized interests) (Olson, 1965; Becker, 1983; Tollison, 1988).

From the agency efficiency perspective, although relevant, the choice between strict liability and the negligence rule loses centrality in favor of a more comprehensive analysis of the institutional law-making design. Consider two situations in which the degree of centralization and the liability rule counterbalance each other. A regime of strict liability enforced in the context of a highly decentralized system would likely generate lower agency costs than a negligence rule applied through a highly centralized adjudication system. For example, in a federal system, one state's enactment of legislation imposing a strict liability rule for injuries caused by a specific type of product would not ensure uniformity across jurisdictions, which would depend on the adoption of the proposal either by each state legislature or by the federal legislature. This is because the effects of decentralization (i.e., decreased returns from rent-seeking and decreased exit option costs) dominate the effects of a move from negligence to strict liability (i.e., reduced uniformity and scope of the law). Conversely, a rule of negligence applied by a centralized adjudicative system would increase the magnitude of influence agency costs more so than a decentralized application of a regime of strict liability would. This is because the effects of centralization (i.e., increased returns from rent-seeking and increased exit option costs) would dominate the effects of a move from strict liability to negligence (i.e., reduced uniformity and scope of the law).

The discussion so far suggests the existence of a trade-off between informational efficiency (which is favored by strict liability) and agency efficiency (which is favored by the negligence rule) in the choice of the liability rule. A process efficiency analysis aims at identifying the institutional variables for choice that optimize this agency/information trade-off. For example, the strictness of the application of the *stare decisis* principle affects the expected duration of the period in which the precedent is likely to remain in force; this increases the expected value of the rents extracted from a favorable legal precedent (Zywicki, 2003). Hence, the sum invested in rent-seeking will increase with increasingly strict applications of the doctrine of precedent. This suggests that, in designing a liability regime in the area of product safety, one might consider exploiting the information cost advantages of strict liability, on th one hand, and mitigating the rent-seeking pressure through a more flexible application of the doctrine precedent, on the other hand.

Sources of Law. I now turn to alternative sources of law in the context of risk regulation. First, the politicization of law-making is likely to increase the magnitude of outcome agency costs[61] The cognitive biases that affect the public perception of risk create opportunities for politicians to extract private benefits from the manipulation of political processes. For example, through the effect of the "availability bias", a highly-publicized, disastrous event may cause an over-estimation of the probability of such an event. (Aviram, 2006, 2007). The poorly intentioned politician could reap the benefits of a public over-estimation of the risk by persuasively overstating the effects of his proposed law and convincing people that the law reduces the likelihood of the disastrous event. In this respect, the adoption of a statutory regime of strict liability would exacerbate the magnitude of outcome agency costs (i.e., costs associated with the manipulation of the outcome). By contrast, a negligence rule, by allocating a portion of law-making power to courts, would counterbalance the distortive effect of politicization.

Second, technocratic law-making entails significant agency costs. As already noted, increased outcome uncertainty leads legislators to enlarge the scope of delegation to agencies, thereby expanding the set of feasible alternatives for agency consideration. This increases outcome agency costs, since the expansion of the regulatory scope of agencies leads to an increasing risk of bureaucratic drift. Delegation in environments characterized by high monitoring costs (often due to information asymmetry, as in the case of risk regulation) increases the costs of reducing agency costs. In response, legislators will set up more constraining regulatory procedures to minimize the risk of bureaucratic drift (McCubbins, 1987; McCubbins et al. 1987).

Courts enjoy comparative advantages in terms of agency efficiency over politics (and bureaucracy). However, such advantages depend on the elasticity of the respective supply curves with respect to external rent-seeking pressures. In fact, while both politics and adjudication supply functions reach a point of *inelasticity* with respect to influence expenditures,[62] "judicial supply curves become inelastic at much lower prices than legislative supply curves do." (Merrill, 1997) The differences in the shapes of the political and judicial supply curves reflect the greater "rent-selling" power of politicians.[63] Namely, the adjudication process

[61] A vast body of economic literature analyzes the agency problems that plague the political process. Here, I briefly mention only those that are specifically related to the area of product safety.

[62] Epstein (1982) that emphasizes the presence of "institutional barriers to effective wealth redistribution through the manipulation of common law rules".

[63] Rent-offering power is the lawmaker's ability to satisfy rent-seekers' demands by influencing the quality of the legal outcome to swing in a preferred direction. An approximate measure of

reaches a limit with regard to the capacity of supplying legal change and accommodates rent-seeking pressures at lower levels of influencing expenditures.[64]

In environmental settings, in which there appear to be unusually high incentives for pressure groups to engage in rent-seeking activities, two instruments are available to mitigate agency costs. One instrument involves moving to a negligence rule, thereby allocating greater law-making activity powers to judges and exploiting the advantages associated with the elasticity differential between the political and judicial supply curves.[65] The negligence rule has the potential to reduce deadweight losses by diminishing the magnitude of influence expenditures sustained under by stakeholders as effect of rent extorsion by politicians. The second agency-cost-reducing strategy could involve lessening the strictness in the application of the principle of *stare decisis*. This suggests that, in contexts with high rent-seeking pressures, if the conditions associated with the informational advantage of strict liability are lacking (e.g., homogeneity of legal demand), the negligence rule is likely to be the "process efficient" rule. By comparison, if the demand is homogeneous and frequent and the incentives to engage in rent-seeking activities are high, the decision between the negligence rule and strict liability will depend on the relative intensities of the two counterbalancing effects (i.e., the information cost reducing effect of strict liability vs. the agency information cost reducing effect of negligence).

Generally, private legal ordering suffers from rent-seeking pressures and related risks of norm manipulation. However, in the area of product safety, the agency costs associated with private law-making are mitigated. First, the reputational element is intensified by the seller-customer relationship between consumers and firms that underlies the demand for product safety. Litigation cases involving product liability receive significant attention in the media, especially when they concern widely sold products (Klein & Leffer, 1981). Moreover, informational

rent-offering power might be the monetary amount of rent that the lawmaker can offer to rent-seekers.

64 Epstein (1982) emphasizes, with respect to the common law system, the presence of "institutional barriers to effective wealth redistribution through the manipulation of common law rules"].

65 The elasticity differential between political and judicial supply curves has two important implications in terms of agency costs. First, when the supply curves reach the point of inelasticity, the influence curves of opposing interest groups become identical. At that point, adjudication becomes unresponsive to any increase in the level of influence expenditures; that is, no group is capable of enhancing its influence power (I assume here that all groups have reached the level of influence expenditures at which the supply curve becomes inelastic). Second, from the aggregate standpoint, when the relative influence powers of pressure groups are neutralized, the amount of resources invested in influence expenditures constitutes a deadweight loss for society.

and reputational cascades may quickly induce changes in the public's perception of risk. Second, monitoring costs are lower because of the large number of consumers involved; thus, wrongful conduct is more likely to be detected. Third, the presence of common regulatory interests among consumers facilitates their coalescence and coordination. This is confirmed by the increasing role played by consumer associations in the policy-making process. All of these environmental conditions facilitate the functioning of private regulatory systems aimed at mitigating the opportunistic behaviors of manufacturing industries.

4.2.3. Adaptive Efficiency

To provide the right signals to firms, the expected costs of legal liability must be *predictable*. Predictable product liability rules increase deterrence by lowering the costs of appreciating the legal consequences of behaviors. At the same time, product liability rules must adapt to changes in the demand for product safety associated with technological innovation. The process efficiency analysis poses the question of which institutional law-making mechanism is best able to deal with the trade-off between predictability and adaptivity.

Predictability: Strict Liability versus Negligence. First, from a predictability standpoint, strict liability appears suited to providing a more stable legal regime. By simplifying the grounds on which cases are decided, strict liability provides a clearer definition and a strict enforcement of property rights, thereby generating a certainty-enhancing effect.[66] Observe, however, that it can be said that strict liability *strictly* enforces property rights only if factual causation is the criterion for the imputation of legal liability (Rizzo, 1980). If factual causation (ie., the question of who has caused the damage) is regarded irrelevant, as in the conventional perspective,[67] than the judge is entitled to allocate liability on the basis of output-oriented efficiency criteria, which depend on several difficult-to-measure (and, therefore, hard to predict) quantitative relationships.

Predictability: Sources of Law. The choice of the source of law also has implications in terms of legal certainty. Some scholars have maintained that scheduled damages and capped damages could increase stability and enhance legal certainty in the application of product liability rules (Danzon, 1992). However, the process efficiency analysis suggests that legal predictability is a function of the quality of the law-making *process,* rather than of the formal characteristics of the legal

---

[66] Counterarguments can be found in Trebilcock (1989).

[67] From a conventional law and economics standpoint, in case of negative externality, the identification of the efficient allocation of property rights is indipendent of the issue of material causation ("who causes the damage"). It rather depends on the identification of the most valued use of the property right ("who values the property right the most").

outcome. Capped or scheduled damages improve the precision of the written rule. However, legal certainty remains impossible to achieve through the legislative process because legislators' incentives to change or maintain existing laws are highly volatile and dependent on the balance of power among competing contingent interest groups.

Adaptivity: Strict Liability versus Negligence. The promulgation of legal rules by a centralized lawmaker provides a focal point around which people can coordinate their compliance decisions (Ribstein, 1992; Gillette, 1998). The enactment of standards of behavior that are *binding* on the whole of the community can support a mass migration to a new Pareto-superior legal equilibrium by reducing the fear of a solitary transition, thus allowing for a "simultaneous movement" to a superior legal regime.[68] In this respect, a regime of strict liability, combined with the centralization of the law-making process (either judicial, administrative, or political) might favor legal change when high information adaption costs impair collective migration of manufacturers to more efficient standards of behavior.

On the other hand, due to high levels of information and agency costs, centralized responses to the demand for legal change are often *slow* to emerge (whether in courts, legislatures, or administrative agencies).[69] Further, centralized law-makers do not internalize the benefits or (most of the) costs of enacted legislation—a reality that contradicts an essential condition of *efficient* legal change. Epstein (1998) vividly summarizes this point: "The centralization of power has the same consequences here [i.e., in a strict product liability regime] that it has in other area of government regulation. It leads to a legal regime that is unresponsive to changes in demand and technology."

Adaptivity: Sources of Law. The analysis of the sources of law provides further insights. Political law-making faces high resistance costs. In fact, the prospective nature of enacted rules imposes a *non*-incremental direction on legal changes and a consequent larger resistance on the part of losers. Resistance arises, in particular, as an effect of the impact of a new product liability regime on

---

68 Due to network externalities, individuals' expected benefit from transiting to a new legal regime depends on the number of people who will adopt it. Efficiency requires that the number of people who adopt the new rule positively affect the benefit of belonging to the new legal network, to the point that the benefits exceed the transition costs.

69 Uniform top-down legal supply systems suffer from informational disadvantages, especially when the supply of law 1) depends on widely dispersed factual knowledge or 2) requires an exploration of innovative legal solutions. By comparison, diversified bottom-up law-making processes ensure a more efficient use of the dispersed information and generate innovative legal solutions as a result of parallel experimentation processes.

products previously placed in the stream of commerce (e.g., many durable or capital goods have long-term risky effects).

Courts enjoy strategic political advantages in terms of adaptive efficiency. First, as already noted, the judicial supply of law becomes inelastic at lower levels of influence expenditures, thereby causing a leveling of the playing field. This proves crucial in the area of product safety, which is usually characterized by strong asymmetries in influencing power between consumers and producers. Second, the fact-specific and *retrospective* nature of judicial decisions enables judges to lower the political visibility of legal changes, thereby lowering the level of resistance costs. Furthermore, the incremental nature of judicial legal change enables individuals to make more accurate estimations of the expected costs of future courses of action. It also reduces the prohibitively high marginal information costs that the synoptic approach postulated by rational choice theory would entail.[70] Furthermore, proceeding through marginal adjustments reduces the risk of errors generated by outcome uncertainty (Sweet, 2002). The preceding considerations might explain why the evolution of the regime of product liability in the U.S. has been, foremost, a creature of judicial action and has moved in the direction of shifting the burden of loss from producers to consumers (Epstein, 1988; Priest, 1991).

However, it must be recognized that judicial decision-making is affected by cognitive biases that affect its ability to properly assess the risk associated with products.[71] Therefore, the improved ability of courts to promote legal change, if combined with environmental settings (as outcome uncertainties) that emphasize these cognitive limitations, might ultimately exacerbate outcome inefficiency. Discussing the prominent role of judicial action in the area of product liability,

[70] In synoptic decision-making, all the information relevant to the decision is gathered and evaluated in light of all of the relevant goals. These goals are clearly identified *ex ante* and weighed according to the decision-maker's values and preferences, which are also clearly identified and prioritized. Every available, rationally conceivable, alternative policy is considered, and the consequences of each possible alternative are weighed according to the identified values, preferences, and goals. By contrast, incremental decision-making begins with a consideration of the status quo, rather than an assessment of every policy alternative. Importantly, the status quo is generally maintained until an existing policy fails, which triggers the need for change and a search for alternatives. Only a restricted number of alternatives is examined, and only a limited range of consequences is weighed. Finally, decisions are continuously adjusted to the feedback generated by the regulatory environment resulting from previous marginal changes.

[71] A number of experimental studies have documented those shortcomings in jury behaviour that discourage the introduction of new products (and novel risks). For example, Moore & Viscusi (1991) provide empirical findings supporting the hypothesis that novel hazards are hit harder than more familiar risks because courts and jurors tend to award larger damages in cases of novel risk-related injuries..

Epstein (1988) observed: "[...] all doctrinal innovation has come from the courts, where the technical lags and information deficits are at their highest."

Most law and economics literature justifies judicial or regulatory intervention in the area of product safety based on the failure of voluntary transactions (Spence, 1977; Epple & Raviv, 1978; Polinsky & Rogerson, 1983; Geistfield, 1995). However, the environmental setting generating the demand for safety provides incentives for the emergence of private legal orderings aimed at mitigating the opportunistic behaviors of manufacturing industries.[72] Furthermore, as has been already noted, private legal orderings enjoy relative advantages in environments characterized by technical complexity and outcome uncertainty, in which the identification of efficient standards of conduct requires the specialized knowledge possessed by economic actors. Interestingly, greater technical complexity (and, thus, greater need for de-centralized sources of information) emerges in more concentrated markets—that is, those markets in which the potential for the self-correction of private markets through self-regulation is stronger (Ramseyer, 1996).

4.3. Summary

The discussion of product safety has exemplified how process efficiency analysis can complement the conventional output-oriented economic approach to legal issues. First, conventional law and economics explains the choice between strict liability and negligence based on the costs and incentives faced by potential injurers and the potential injured. By contrast, process efficiency analysis suggests that this choice is better explained in terms of the impact on law-making costs. In fact, strict liability increases the uniformity and scope of the application of the law, thereby accentuating the ex-ante centralized dimension of law making. In terms of information efficiency, strict liability proves efficient when the demand for law is highly homogeneous and frequent. In addition, when both aggregate frequency and frequency per actor are relatively high, the relative advantages of strict liability in terms of lower information cost are magnified. In short, a move from negligence to strict liability intensifies the economizing effect associated with ex-ante centralization by increasing the uniformity of the supply and breadth of the scope of the law.

---

[72] The insistence by the majority of law and economics scholarship on the centralized form of intervention is a form of Nirvana fallacy: The imperfection of the market is *per se* sufficient to justify a call for other idealized sources of law. By contrast, a careful process efficiency analysis requires a comparative investigation of the relative abilities of alternative law-making mechanisms to improve efficiency.

Second, with respect to agency efficiency, a regime of strict liability is likely to increase agency costs both in terms of rent-seeking costs and outcome agency costs; conversely, a regime of negligence allows for decreased agency costs due to the advantages of adjudication in terms lessened rent-selling power. Process efficiency analysis illuminates a trade-off between information costs and agency costs, which is generally overlooked by conventional output oriented analysis. Finally, with regard to adaptive efficiency, a regime of strict liability is likely to slow the responsiveness of the law to changes in legal environments.

Third, and perhaps more importantly, process efficiency analysis identifies a number of institutional variables whose impact in terms of efficiency is far more profound than the move from negligence to strict liability. The effect of changes in the degree of centralization in law-making institutional design is likely to dominate the effects of changes in the regime of liability. A move from a negligence rule to a strict liability regime exerts different impacts on the law-making cost structure (at both the process and the output level) depending on the overall organization of the sources of law. For example, a regime of strict liability enforced in the context of a highly decentralized system would likely generate lower agency costs than a negligence rule applied through a highly centralized adjudication system. This is because the effects of decentralization (a decreased return from rent seeking and decreased exit option costs) would dominate the effects of a move from negligence to strict liability (reduced uniformity and width of the scope of the law).

Fourth, conventional law and economics tends to overlook the choice of the institutional mechanisms that are adopted to define the legal standard of care. For example, the traditional debate on ex-post tort liability versus ex-ante safety standards is output-oriented in that it focuses on the incentive structure faced by potential injurers and injured. This perspective tends to miss the important understanding that the ex-ante and ex-post dimension of law making affects both the structure of law-making costs and the content of alternative classes of rules due to the differences in alternative sources of law in terms of information, agency, and adaptive efficiency. On the contrary, as repeatedly emphasized, process efficiency analysis illuminates the relative advantages and disadvantages in terms of the efficiency of courts, legislatures, administrative agencies, and private organizations.

Process efficiency illuminates the importance of institutional choice in those areas where riskiness and outcome uncertainty are relatively high. In these cases, the choice of the institutional decision-making mechanism has a dramatic impact on the liability regime. The choice of the law maker is probably more salient in determining the efficiency of the law than the choice between strict liability and the negligence rule. Process efficiency analysis suggests that under certain conditions, shifting portions of law-making powers to private legal orderings might generate significant efficiency advantages in tailoring the regulatory intervention to redress the informational failures of the unregulated market.

The Japanese product liability system, which was in force until 1995, represents a significant historical example of a nongovernmental product liability system. Until 1995, product liability in Japan was formally subject to a general negligence regime. Despite this form of legal regime, many Japanese firms had incentives to offer insurance coverage as a signal to buyers of the quality and safety of their products and agreed to be subject to a regime of strict liability. The enforcement mechanism was based on a centralized public authority, but the creation of the liability regime was activated by the spontaneous choices of manufacturing industries (Ramseyer, 1996).

In conclusion, process efficiency analysis provides a different perspective on the three issues mentioned above and also reconsiders their actual relevance relative to the more general organizational framework of the sources of law. As to *issue 1*, the move from negligence to strict liability is viewed as one that increases the uniformity and scope of the application of the law, thereby affecting the structure and magnitude of law-making costs. *Issue 2* is misplaced; the question is not whether the market could efficiently regulate the area of product safety but rather which of the available institutional law-making alternatives enhances efficiency in the area of product safety depending on the specific characteristics of the demand for safety. As to *issue* 3, the choice between ex-post tort liability or ex-ante safety standards depends on the structure of law-making costs (with regard to specific objects of regulation) rather than on the incentives of relevant actors at the margin.

5. CONCLUSIONS

I have investigated several issues in this paper. First, I have argued that an output bias underlies conventional law and economics methodology. The structural features of the legal environment contradict, in many important respects, the assumptions underlying conventional models. To overcome these shortcomings, this paper has argued that the efficiency of the law is better explained as a function of the institutional and structural variables that affect the law formation mechanisms (rather than the allocation of legal entitlements insulated from the law-making process). Efficiency is not an objective property of the outcome independent of the process; rather, it depends on the ability of the law-making process to embody, in a cost-effective manner, the general consensus of all the people concerned. Individuals consent to the "process-outcome relationship" rather than to an idealized output insulated from the law-making process. They choose the best possible process–outcome ratio: the one that enhances their own welfare while minimizing the costs of reaching consensus, under the constraint of the preferences of others and the conditions of the *status quo*. The outcome attained is not "optimal" in the standard Paretian sense but is "optimally" produced.

Second, to enable the assessment of alternative law-making mechanisms, I have introduced the notion of process efficiency. The law-making process is efficient if there is no alternative institution that does better across the circumstances in which it actually operates in producing legal rules such that each member of society is enabled to enhance his or her own welfare. The comparative assessment of alternative sources of law is based on the structure of the transaction costs associated with each law-making mechanism under changing environmental settings. For this purpose, I have proposed a unified taxonomy of law-making costs based on the three components of process efficiency: information efficiency, agency efficiency, and adaptive efficiency. The analysis of the variables affecting law-making costs is organized for each category of costs along the lines of a supply and demand model. The supply side summarizes the features of the law-making process that are predicted to mostly affect the structure of law-making costs The demand side summarizes the exogenous conditions of the regulated environments. Each category of cost includes demand side costs, supply side costs, and an "outcome" dimension (see *supra* figure 2). Thus, the outcome is not eschewed by the efficiency analysis; rather, it is conceptualized as a function of the incentive structure underlying the law-making process.

Third, the discussion on product safety has illustrated more concretely how process efficiency analysis can complement the conventional output oriented economic approach to legal issues. The move from negligence to strict liability is viewed as one that increases the uniformity and scope of the supply of law, thereby affecting the structure and magnitude of law-making costs. Generally, strict liability is justified when the demand for safety exhibits high levels of both homogeneity and frequency of the legal demand. There is a trade-off between information and agency costs. The optimization of this trade-off is related to the degree of centralization in the overall organization of the sources of law and with the degree of strictness of the doctrine of precedent. The choice between ex-post tort liability and ex-ante safety standards also affects the structure of law-making costs. In this respect, process efficiency analysis illuminates the relative advantages and disadvantages of ex-ante centralized processes versus ex-post decentralized processes in the definition of the optimal standards of care. It also emphasizes the relative advantages of private legal orderings in the creation of legal rules in areas characterized by technical complexity, outcome uncertainty, and relatively high rates of change.

REFERENCES

Adler, M. D. (2000). Beyond Efficiency and Procedure: A Welfarist Theory of Regulation. *Florida State Law Review*, *28*, 241.

Adler, M. D., & Posner, E. A. (1999). Rethinking Cost-Benefit Analysis. *Yale Law Journal*, *109*, 165.

Aranson, P. H., Gellhorn, E., & Robinson, G. O. (1982). Theory of Legislative Delegation. *Cornell Law Review*, *68*, 1.

Arlen, J. (2010). Contracting Over Liability; Medical Malpractice and the Cost of Choice. *University of Pennsylvania Law Review*, 957.

Ausness, R. C. (2000). Waive Goodbye to Tort Liability: A Proposal to remove Paternalism from Product SalesTransactions. *San Diego Law Review*, *37*, 293.

Aviram, A. (2007). Bias Arbitrage. *Washington & Lee Law Review*, *64*, 789.

Aviram, A. (2006). The Placebo Effect of Law: Law's Role in Manipulating Perceptions. *George Washington Law Review* (75).

Bebchuck, L. A. (1980). The Pursuit of a Bigger Pie. Can Everyone Expect a Bigger Pie? *Hostra Law Review*, 672.

Becker, G. (1983). A Theory of Competition among Pressure Groups for Political Influence. *The Quarterly Journal of Economics*, *98*.

Ben-Shahar, O. (1998). Should Product Liability be based on Hindsight? *Journal of law, Economics and Organization*, *14*, 325.

Bernstein, L. (1992). Opting out of the Legal System: Extralegal Contractual Relations in the Diamond Industry. *The Journal of Legal Studies*, *21* (1), 115.

Bertrand, E. (2014). The Fugitive: The Figure of Judges in Coasean Economics. *Journal of Institutional Economics*, *1*.

Bodway, R. W., & Bruce, N. (1984). *Welfare Economics.* B. Blackwell.

Bremer, E. S. (2013). Incorporation by Reference in an Open-Government Age. *Harvard Journal of law and Public Policy*, *36* (1), 131.

Breyer, S. (2009). *Breaking the Vicious Circle: Toward Effective Risk Regulation.* St.

Paul: Thompson Reuters.

Buchanan, J. (1977). *Freedom in Constitutional Contract.* College Station: Texas A&M University Press.

Buchanan, J. M., & Tullock, G. (1965). *The Calculus of Consent: Logical Foundations of Constituional Democracy.* Ann Arbor: University of Michigan Press.

Buchanan, J. (1959). Positive Economics, Welfare Economics, and Political Economy. *Journal of law and Economics* (2).

Buchanan, J. (1984). Rights, Efficiency and Exchange. In *Anspruche, Eigentums und Verfungungsrechte.* Berlin: Dunker und Humblot.

Buchanan, J. (1975). *The Limits of Liberty.* Chicago: The University of Chicago Press.

Buchanan, J. (1962). The Relevance of Pareto Optimality. *Journal of Conflict Resolution , 6.*

Calabresi, G. (1991). The Pointlessness of Pareto: Carrying Coase Further. *Yale law Journal , 100,* 1227.

Champman, B. (2005). Economic Analaysis of Law and the value of Efficiency. In A. N. Hatzis, *Economic Analysis of Law: A Europena Perspective* (S. 4-5). Cheltenham: Elgar.

Choi, A. H., & Spier, K. E. (2013). Should Consumers be Permitted to Waive Product Liability? Product safety, Private Contracts and Adverse Selection. *Harvard Law and Economics Discussion Paper* , 680.

Cirillo, R. (1979). *The Economics of Vilfredo pareto.* London: Frank Cass.

Coleman, J. (1980). Efficiency, Exchange and Auction: Philosophic Aspects of the Economic Approach to Law. *California Law Review , 68,* 226-31.

Coleman, J. L. (1980). Efficiency, Utility and Wealth Maximization. *Hofstra Law Review , 8,* 515-20.

Coleman, J. L. (1985). Market Contractarianism and the Unanimity Rule. *Social Philosophy and Policy , 2* (2), 69.

Coleman, J. L. (1987). *Markets Morals and the Law.* Doerdecht: D. Reidel Publishing Co.

Cooter, R. D. (1992). Structural Adjudication and the New Law Merchant: A Model of Decentralized Law. *International Review of law and Economics , 21*

(1), 115.

Cooter, R., & Ulen, T. (2008). *Law and Economics*. Glenview: Illinois, Ecott, Foresman.

Danzon, P. M. (1992). Tort Reform and the Role of Government in Private Insurance Markets. *Journal of Legal Studies* (8), 273.

Dari-Mattiacci, G., & Deffains, B. (2007). Uncertainty of Law and the Legal Process. *Journal of Instituional and Theoretical Law and Economics* .

Daughety, A. F., & Reinganum, J. F. (1995). Product Safety: Liabilty, R&D, and Signaling. *American Economic Review* , *85*, 1187.

Ellerman, D. (2009). Numeraire Illusion. The Final Demise of Kaldor-Hicks Principle. In T. F. Economics, & M. D. White (Hrsg.). Cambridge: Cambridge University Press.

Ellickson, R. (1991). *Order Without Law. How Neighbors Settle Disputes.* Cambridge, Massachusset: Harvard University Press.

Epple, D., & Raviv, A. (1978). Product Safety: Liability Rules, Market Structure, and Imperfect Information. *American Economic Review* , *68*, 80.

Epstein, R. (1982). The Social Consequences of Common Law Rules. *Harvard Law Review* , *95* (8), 1717.

Epstein, R. (1988). The Unintended Revolution in Product Liability Law. *Cardozo law Review* , *10*, 2202.

Fraiberg, J., & Trebilock, M. J. (1997). Risk regulation: Technocratic and Democratic Tools for Regulatory Reform. *McGill Law Journal* , *43*, 835.

Garoupa, N., & Gomez, L. C. (2011). Syndrom of the Efficiency of Common Law. *Boston University International law Journal* , *29*, 287.

Geistfield, M. (1995). Manufacturer Moral Hazard and the Tort-Contract Issue in Products Liability. *International Review of Law and Economics* , *15*, 241.

Gillette, C. P. (1998). Lock-in Effects in law and Norms. *Boston University Law Review* , *78*, 813.

Goldberg, J. C., & Zipursky, B. C. (2010). The Easy Case for Products Liability Law: A Response to Professor Polinsky and Shavell. *Harvard Law Review* , *123*.

Guthrie, C., Rachlinski, J. J., & Wistrich, A. J. (2001). Inside the Judicial Mind.

Cornell Law Review , *86*, 777.

Guthrie, C., Rachlinski, J. J., & Wistrich, A. J. (2001). Inside The Judicial Mind. *Cornell Law Review* , *86*, 777.

Hadfield, G. K. (1992). Bias in the Evolution of Legal Rules. *The Georgetown Law Journal* , *80*, 583-616.

Harsanyi, J. C. (1978). Bayesian Decision Theory and Utilitarian Ethics. *The American Economic Review* , *68* (2).

Hicks, J. R. (1941). The Rehabilitation of Consumer's Surplus. *Review of Economic Studies* , *8*, 108.

J.Miceli, T. (1997). *Economics of the Law.* Oxford, UK: Oxford University Press.

Kaldor, N. (1939). Welfare Propositions of Economic and Interpersonal Comparisons of Utility. *Economic Jpurnal* (49), 549.

Kaplow, L. (1986). An Economic Analysis of Legal Transitions. *Harvard Law Review* , *99* (3), 509-617.

Klein, B., & Leffer, K. B. (1981). The Role of market Forces in Assuring Contractual Performance. *Journal of Political Economy* , *89*, 615.

Kolstad, C., Ulen, T. S., & Johnson, G. V. (1990). Ex Post Liability for Harm vs. Ex Ante Safety Regulation: Substitutes or Complements? *The American Economic Review* , *80* (4), 888.

Komesar, N. (1994). *Imperfect Alternatives. Choosing Institutions in Law, Economics and Public Policy.* Chicago: The University of Chicago Press.

Langlois, R., & Csontos, L. (1983). Optimization, Rule Following and the Methodology of Situational Analaysis. In B. G. Uskali maki, *Rationality, Institutions and Economic Methodology.* New York: Routledge.

Le Grand, J. (1991). *Equity and Choice. An Essay in Economics and Applied Philosophy.* London: Harper Collins Academic.

Leff, A. A. (1976). Economic Analaysis of Law: Some Realism About Nominalism. *Virginia Law review* , *60*, 451.

Markovits, R. S. (1993). Constructive Critique of the Traditional Definition and Use of the Concept of the Effect of a Choice on Allocative (Economic) Efficiency. *University of Illinois Law Review* , 485.

Mathis, K. (2009). *Efficiency instead of Justice? Searching for the Philosophical Foundations of the Economic Analysis of Law.* Springer.

McChesney, F. S. (1997). *Money for Nothing: Politicians, Rent Extraction, and Political Extortion.* Cambridge, Massachussets: Harvard University Press.

McChesney, F. S. (1987). Ret Extraction and rent Creation in the Economic Theory of Regulation. *The Journal of Legal Studies , 16*, 101.

McCubbins, M. D. (1985). The Legisaltive Design of Regulatory Structure. *American Journal of Political Science , 29* (4), 721.

McCubbins, M. D., Noll, R. G., & Weingast, B. R. (1987). Administrative Procedures as Instruments of Political Control. *Journal of Law, Economics, and Organization , 243* (3).

Mercuro, N., & Medema, S. G. (1997). *Economics and the Law: form Posner to Post-Modernism.* Princeton: Princeton University Press.

Mercuro, N., & Ryan, T. R. (1984). *Law Economics and Public Policy.* Greenwich: JAI Press.

Merrill, T. W. (1997). Does Public Choice Theory Justifies Activism After All. *Harvard Law Journal and Public Policy , 21*, 219.

Miceli, T. J. (1997). *Economics of the Law.* Oxford: Oxford University Press.

Miceli, T. J., Rabon, R., & Segerson, K. (2013). Liability Regulation for Product-Related Risk. In T. J. Miceli, & M. J. Baker, *Research Handbook on Economic Models of Law.* Cheltenham: Edward Elgar.

Mishan, E. J. (1967). Pareto Optimality and the Law. *Oxford Economic Papers , 19.*

Mitnick, B. M. (1980). *The Political Economy of Regulation: Creating, Designing and Removing Regulaotry Forms.* New York: Columbia University Press.

Moore, M. J., & Viscusi, K. W. (1991). An Industrial Profile of the Links Between Product Liability and Innovation. In H. P. W., & R. E. Litan, *The Liability Maze: The Impact of Liability Law on Safety and Innovation.* Washington: The Brooking Institution.

Muller, C. (2004). The Methodology of Contractarianism in Economics. *Public Choice , 113* (3-4).

O'Hara, E. A., & Ribstein, L. E. (2000). From Politics to Efficiency of Choice of Law. *The University of Chicago Law Review , 67*, 1151.

Olson, M. (1965). *The Logic of collectgive Action: Public Goods and the Theory of Groups.*

Harvard University Press.

Ostrom, E. (2005). *Understanding Instituional Diversity*. Princeton: Princeton University Press.

Parisi, F. (2004). Positive, Normative and Functional Schools in Law and Economics. *European Journal of Law and Economics , 18* (3), 259.

Parisi, F. Sources of Law and the Instituional Design of Law-making. *Journal of Public Finance and Public Choice , 2-3*, 95-122.

Parisi, F. (1995). Toward a Theory of Spontaneous Law. *Constituional Political Economy , 6* (3).

Parisi, F., & Fon, V. (2009). *The Economics of Lawmaking*. Oxford: Oxford University Press.

Patchel, K. (1993). Interest Group Politics, Federalism, and the Uniform Laws Process: Some Lessons from the Uniform Commercial Code. *Minnesota Law Review , 78*, 83.

Polinsky, M. A. (2003). *An Introduction to law and Economics* (3th edition Ausg.). New York, US: Aspen Publishers.

Polinsky, M., & Rogerson, W. P. (1983). Products Liability, Consumer Misperceptions, and Market Power. *Bell of Journal Economics , 14*, 581.

Posner, R. (1992). *Economic Analysis of Law* (4th edition Ausg.). Boston: Little, Brown.

Priest, G. (1981). A Theory of the Consumer Product Damages. *Yale Law Journal , 90.*

Priest, G. (1991). The ModernExpansion of Tort Laibility: Its Sources, its Effects, and Its Reform. *Journal of Economic Perspectives , 5*, 31.

Quinn, J., & Trebilcock, M. J. (1982). Compensation, Transition Costs and Regulaotry Change. *University of Toronto law Journal , 32* (2), 117.

Rachlinski, J. J. (1998). Regulating in Foresight Versus Judging Liability in Hindsight: The Case of Tobacco. *Ga. L. review , 33*, 813.

Ramseyer, M. J. (1996). Products Liability through Private Ordering: Notes on a Japanese Experiment . *University of Pennsylvania Law Review* (144), 1823.

Rawls, J. (1971). *A Theiry of Justice*. Cambridge, Massachussets: Harvard University press.

Redoano, M. (2010). Does centralization Affect The Number and Size of Lobbies? *Journal of Public Economic Theory* , *12* (3), 407.

Ribstein, L. (1992). Choosing Law By Contract. *Journal of Corporate Law* , 273.

Ribstein, L. E., & Kobayashi, B. (1996). An Economic Analysis of Uniform State Laws. *Journal of Legal Studies* , *25*, 131.

Rizzo, M. (1980). Law Amid Flux: The Economics of Negligence and Strict Liability in Tort. *Journal of Legal Studies* , 291-318.

Samuels, W. J. (1981). Maximization of Wealth as Justice: an Essay on Posnerian law and Economics as Policy Analysis. *Texas law Review* , *60*, 150.

Samuels, W. J. (1 1978). Normative Premises in Regulatory Theory. *Journal of Post-Keynesian Economics* , 102-104.

Samuels, W. J., & Mercuro, N. (1984). Posnerian Law and Economics on the Bench. *International Review of Law and Economics* (4).

Schmid, A. A. (2004). Conflict and Cooperation. Instituional and Behavioral Economics.

Schmid, A. A. (1989). Law and Economics: An Institutional Perspective. In N. Mercuro, *Law and Economics* (S. 68-69). Boston: Kluwer Academic Publishers.

Schmid, A. A., & Shaffer, J. D. (1964). Marketing in Social Perspective. In V. L. Sorenson, *Agricaltural Market Analysis.* East Lansing: Michigan State University.

Schmitz, P. W. (2000). On the Joint Use of Liabillity and safety Regulation. *International Review of Law and Economics* , *20*, 371.

Schwartz, A. (1992). The Case Against Strict Liability. *Fordham Law Review* , *60*, 819.

Scitovsky, T. (1941). A Note on Welfare Propositions in Economics. *Review of Economic Studies* , *9* (77).

Sen, A. K. (1970). *Collective Choice and Social Welfare.* Amsterdam: Holden-Day Inc.

Shavell, S. (2004). *Foundations of Economic Analysis of Law.* Cambridge, MA: The Belknap Press of Harvard University Press.

Shavell, S. (1984). Liability for Harm versus Regulation of Safety. *Journal of Legal Studies* , *13*, 357.

Shavell, S. (1980). Strict Liability Versus Negligence. *Journal of Legal Studies , 9.*

Spence, M. (1977). Consumer Misperceptions, Product Failure and Producer Liability. *Review of Economic Studies , 44*, 561.

Stearns, M. L., & Todd, Z. (2009). *Public Choice Concepts and Applications in Law.* Thompson Reuters.

Sunstein, C. R. (1996). The Cost-Benefit State. *(39)* .

Sweet, A. S. (2002). *Judicialization and the Construction of Governance.* Oxford: Oxfrod University Press.

Tollison, R. (1988). Public Choice and Legislation. *Virginia law Review , 74*, 339.

Trebilcock, M. J. (2014). *Dealing with Losers. The Political Economy of Policy Transitions.* Oxford: Oxford University Press.

Trebilcock, M. J. (1989). The Future of Tort Law: Mapping the Contours of the Debate. *Canadian Businness Law Journal , 15*, 471.

Trebilcock, M. J. (1975). Winners and Losers in the Modern Regulaotry System: Must the Consumer Always Lose? *Osgoode Hall Law Journal* (13), 619.

Tullock, G. (1975). The Transitional Gain Trap. *The Bell Journal of Economics , 6* (2).

Twight, C. (1994). Political Transaction-Cost Manipulation: An Integrating Theory. *Journal of Theoretical Politics , 6* (2).

Ulen, R. C. (2008). *Law and Economics* (5th edition Ausg.). Glennview, Illinois: Scott, Foresman.

Veljanovski, C. G. (1980). The Economic Approach to Law: A Critical Introduction. *Britisj Journal of Law and Society , 7*, 158.

Viscusi, K. W. (2000). *Corporate Risk Analysis: A reckless Act?* Discussion Paper, Harvard Law School.

Zywicki, T. (2003). The Rise and Fall of Efficiency in the Common Law: A Supply-Side Analysis. *Northwestern University Law Review , 97* (4), 1551.

TIMELY AND NECESSARY: ECOCIDE LAW AS URGENT AND EMERGING.

Bronwyn Lay, PhD, European Graduate School

Laurent Neyret, Professor of Law, University of Versailles

Damien Short, Reader of Human Rights,
Director Human Rights Consortium, University of London

Michael Urs Baumgartner, MSW, Greenpeace, Switzerland

Antonio A. Oposa Jr, International Visiting Professor, University of Hawai'i

INTRODUCTION:

This paper explores an international law of ecocide, which at its simplest is the mass damage and destruction of the environment resulting from human action. The renowned Indian jurist M.C. Mehta stated in the recently released Oslo Principles on Global Climate Change Obligations the following guide for those engaged in legal processes: "When our legal systems become overly technical and convoluted they can stray too far from reality. Lawyers and the courts must see to it that their interpretations of the law adhere to reality as closely as possible. Otherwise legal systems become rudderless and stray, from that single trajectory, which must be towards justice, into technicalities."[1] While technical complexity and political questions have become increasingly understood as law, our current ecological crisis asks profound legal questions and for the re-emergence of legal reasoning, rather than technical translation. This paper will focus on the deeper, increasingly ignored, role of law to use reason and judgement in interpreting and guiding the major issues of our times and briefly justifies why a law of ecocide is a legal imperative.

[1] http://www.yale.edu/macmillan/globaljustice/Oslo%20Principles.pdf

The vital principle of *nulla poena sine lege* articulates that there is no penalty without law. While there are many interpretations of this in international law, in this case it speaks to the reality that there is no law against criminal mass damage and destruction of ecosystems in peacetime. At this historical juncture of climate change and environmental destruction this omission seems like legalised madness and violence. Ecocide challenges international law and asks it to fulfil its mandate of law beyond nation state sovereignty regarding environmental destruction. As one influential judge at the International Criminal Court stated when asked about the viability of ecocide law, 'rather than anything else it will mainly take courage.' The Oslo Principles state that avoiding severe global catastrophe is both a moral and legal imperative.[2]

Since the 1990s a whole area of criminological scholarship, termed environmental or 'green' criminology, has emerged that seeks to identify important environmental harms and draws attention to their impacts for humans, non-human animals and ecosystems more generally as well as their causes and potential remedial action, including the criminalisation of such otherwise 'legal' harms.[3] This body of scholarship has recently considered the necessity of a law prohibiting ecocide and concluded that such a law is necessary and arguably essential to protect the planet and its ecosystems from destruction.[4] Embracing this argument, this paper attempts to place a law of ecocide within emerging jurisprudences where the criminalisation of ecocide will take place because it must, and briefly outlines the jurisprudential support for its inclusion as an international crime in peace and war. Some crimes are so self-evidently wrong, morally and legally, that efforts to shackle such crimes to overly technical application and execution renders them devoid of utility from the perspective of protecting the

---

[2] Ibid.

[3] Higgins, P, Short, D and South, N (2013) 'Protecting the Planet: A proposal for a law of ecocide, *Crime, Law and Social Change*, 59, No1.

[4] Ibid.

environment. No area of law is an island and ecocide is a vital part of an emergent jurisprudence that clarifies the duty of care towards the environment.

WHAT IS ECOCIDE?

Outside a legal definition, ecocide is any extensive damage or destruction of the natural landscape and disruption or loss of ecosystems of a given territory to such an extent that the survival of the inhabitants of that territory is endangered. The term ecocide was born from science. The plant biologist and chair of the Department of Botany at Yale University Arthur Galston first publicly used the term ecocide in 1970 after researching herbicides. David Zierler's 2011 book *The Invention of Ecocide* traces how the use of herbicidal warfare in the Vietnam war led to the defoliation of large areas of that country and resulted in a movement of scientists who advocated for ecocide to be an international crime.[5] This was the first known time the crime of ecocide was named, explored and advocated for, yet the political arena failed to respond to the scientific community's witnessing and evidence of the reality of environmental destruction.

Since the Vietnam War, the last fifty years has seen advocacy from influential legal scholars for ecocide to be included as a crime against peace, including the intention for it to be included in the Rome Statute until a last minute removal, which occurred without prior discussions. This process has been outlined by the University of London's Human Rights Consortium report of 2012.[6] Also the 2013 publication of the Science Po report on Ecocide outlines and clarifies the majority of the research and scholarship around

[5] Zierler, David. *The Invention of Ecocide: Agent Orange, Vietnam and the scientists who changed the way we think about the environment*, The University of Georgia Press, London, 2011.

[6] A draft ecocide Convention was submitted in 1973 into the UN and ecocide was included in the draft Rome statute as both a peace-time and war time crime.

legally defining ecocide.[7] Gray, Beret and Higgins have proposed definitions of ecocide. Beret focuses upon geocide as a counterpart to genocide and species destruction is central to her definition.[8] Mark Gray states that three conditions need to be met for ecocide: serious extensive or long lasting ecological damage that has an international dimension and is wasteful. Higgins defines ecocide as the extensive damage to, destruction of or loss of ecosystems of a given territory, whether by human agency or by other causes, to such an extent that peaceful enjoyment by the inhabitants of that territory has been or will be severely diminished. [9] All of them hold individuals with superior responsibility accountability as per all international crimes, and Higgins and Gray agree that it be a strict liability crime which is widely used in many jurisdictions. More recently Neyret has proposed that crimes of ecocide are intentional acts that threaten the security of the planet and are committed as part of a widespread or systematic action, and this definition is refined by reference to specific dangerous activities.[10] These definitions of ecocide have their critics that this paper doesn't have the

[7] M. Garin, B. Glasenhardt, R. Houston, J. Pham, *Report on the ecocide project*, Law Clinic- Sciences Po Paris, 7 December 2013 : http://www.sciencespo.fr/ecole-de-droit/sites/sciencespo.fr.ecole-de-droit/files/rapport_ecocide_project.pdf

[8] Beret defines geocide as "intentional destruction, in whole or in part, of any portion of the global ecosystem, via killing members of a species: causing serious bodily or mental harm to members of the species; inflicting on the species conditions of life that bring about its physical destruction in whole or in part: and imposing measures that prevent births within the group or lead to birth defects. Lynn Berat, "Defending the right to a healthy environment: toward a crime of geocide in international law", *Boston university International Law Journal* (1993) (pp.327-348)

[9] With others Higgins proposes the use of the existing laws of war be extended to peacetime activities in the 1977 United Nations Convention on the Prohibition of Military or any other Hostile Use of Environment Modification Techniques (ENMOD) which defines the terms 'widespread, long lasting and severe as:

a) widespread: encompassing an area on the scale of a several hundred square kilometres.
b) long lasting: lasting for a period of months, or approximately a season.
c) severe: involving serious or significant disruption or harm to human life, natural and economic resources or other assets.

[10] L. Neyret dir., *Des écocrimes à l'écocide, le droit penal au secours de l'environnement*, Bruylant, 2015, p. 288 :
"Ecocide" means any of the following intentional acts when they threaten the security of the planet and are committed as part of a widespread or systematic action:

a. the discharge, emission or introduction of a quantity of substances or ionizing radiation into air or the atmosphere, soil, water or aquatic environments;

scope to explore. Needless to say definitions are emerging, being refined and ultimately it's the responsibility of member states to do the work of definition.

Ecocide law has been proposed as inclusively applying to peacetime as well as wartime, aimed at prosecution of individuals rather than state bodies and therefore also addresses those engaged in non-state activities such as those individuals within transnational corporations who hold positions of superior responsibility.[11] This has been called unprecedented however individual accountability is an ancient principle of criminal law and there is precedent for prosecuting directors and other non-military leaders within international and national criminal jurisdictions.[12] Balthazar Garzon, a senior advisor to

---

b. the collection, transport, recovery or disposal of waste, including the supervision of such operations, and the after-care of disposal sites, including action taken as a dealer or a broker in any activity in relation to waste management;
c. the operation of a plant in which a dangerous activity is carried out or in which dangerous substances or preparations are stored or used;
d. the production, processing, handling, use, holding, storage, transport, import, export or elimination of nuclear materials or other hazardous radioactive substances;
e. the killing, destruction, possession or taking of specimens of wild fauna or flora species whether protected or not;
f. other acts of a similar nature which are committed intentionally and threaten the security of the planet.

2. The acts referred to in paragraph 1 threaten the security of the planet when they cause:
   a. widespread, long-term and severe damage to air or the atmosphere, soil, water, aquatic environments, fauna or flora, or to their ecological functions; or
   b. death, permanent disabilities or serious, incurable diseases to a population or cause a population to be dispossessed of its lands, territories or resources on a lasting basis.
3. The acts referred to in paragraph 1 must be committed intentionally and in the knowledge of the widespread or systematic character of the action of which they are part. Such acts are also considered intentional when their author knew or should have known that there was a high probability that they would threaten the security of the planet.

[11] Article 8(2)(b)(iv) of the Rome Statute prohibits intentionally launching an attack in the knowledge that such attack will cause incidental loss of life or injury to civilians or damage to civilian objects or widespread, long term and severe damage to the non-human environment which would be clearly excessive in relation to the concrete and direct overall military advantage anticipated. Therefore there is provision for the prosecution of ecocide within the Rome Statute but only within wartime. There have been calls to strengthen this provision within wartime most recently from Prof. Steven Freeland. Freeland, S. (2015), '*Addressing the Intentional Destruction of the Environment During Warfare Under the Rome Statute of the International Criminal Court*', : Intersentia 9781780683140.

[12] There is precedent for prosecuting directors and other non-military leaders for aiding and abetting and/or conspiracy charges of genocide/crimes against humanity/war crimes such as Wilhelm Frick in the Nuremberg trials. The removal of the corporate veil is well establish in most standard corporations

the ICC, expert criminal law practitioner and pioneer of universal jurisdiction is currently arguing that this doctrine of accountability extend to corporate crime.[13]

Despite legal and civil society advocacy for half a century, and the presence of ecocide law in at least ten national jurisdictions, international criminal law has been resistant to the inclusion of ecocide within its canon with the exception of the never used provisions in the Rome Statute regarding environmental damage in wartime.[14] This is despite solid historical and extant national legal and moral foundations for its inclusions, the least of which is that humanity depends upon ecosystems for survival. [15]

Like all new laws, to legally define ecocide might be a long journey. However genocide, obviously a crime, was once a moral crime without precedent or legal articulation but wasn't quickly defined as an international crime in the Convention on the Prevention and Punishment of the Crime of Genocide (CPPCG). In 1946, after the evident horrors of the Holocaust, the first session of the United Nations General Assembly adopted a resolution that affirmed that genocide was a crime under international law, but did not provide a legal definition of the crime.[16] Eventually genocide as a jus cogens norm, therefore a fundamental overriding principles of international law from which no derogation is ever permitted, was defined, clarified and incorporated into international

legislation used since the 19th century where offences by officers of bodies corporate are liable for offences committed by the body corporate.

[13] Also the renowned Spanish judge Balthasar Garzon has made recent comments of a positive nature, in his role as advisor to ICC, on the subject of trans boundary corporate responsibility. See http://www.theguardian.com/world/2015/aug/20/spain-judge-baltasar-garzon-prosecute-global-corporations

[14] Ten nations already have existing domestic ecocide law including Georgia, Republic of Armenia, Ukraine, Belarus, Kazakstan, Kyrgzstan, Republic of Moldova, Russian Federation, Tajikistan, Uzbekistan, and Vietnam.

[15] Equally, the myopia of law to address the greatest threat to humanity at this historic juncture, a reality most strongly expressed in science, may result in the collapse of law as a norm bearing and protective instrument.

[16] In 1948, the UN General Assembly adopted the *Convention on the Prevention and Punishment of the Crime of Genocide* (CPPCG).

law to the point that the jurisdiction of the International Criminal Court (ICC) is now based upon that original work. [17] International crimes affect the peace or safety of more than one state or are so reprehensible in nature and extent as to justify the intervention of international agencies in the investigation and prosecution thereof.[18] Genocide and ecocide address different forms of harm: one is directed at social groups, the other at the dependence of humanity upon eco-systems.[19] They can both result in similar amounts of death and destruction, and potential prosecution rests upon both criminal and human rights jurisprudence. At this juncture what is essential is the moral recognition that ecocide should be an international crime, and that resultant processes are set in motion for its incorporation into law.

EMERGING JURISPRUDENCE.

Ecocide law is not a radical expansion of the foundations of western law, and nor does it threaten to undermine these foundations. If anything, it is a natural progression and response to immediate and long-term consequences of harm on a significant scale.[20] While more recent ecocide law advocates base their arguments upon the rights of nature and earth law, more traditional jurisprudence such as constitutional and criminal law also opens ecocide law into the international law constellation, which has been explored in the work of Christian Tomuschat, Mark Drumbl, Richard Falk and Mark Gray among

[17] *See* Ian Brownlie, Principles of Public International Law (5th ed., Oxford, 1998).

[18] "Conservation crime can be defined as any intentional or negligent human activity or manipulation that impacts negatively on the earths biotic and/or abiotic natural resources, resulting in immediately noticeable or indiscernible natural resource trauma of any magnitude." Ed. Rob White, Environmental Crime: A Reader, Willan Publishing, Devon, 2009.

[19] Higgins, P, Short, D and South, N (2013) 'Protecting the Planet: A proposal for a law of ecocide, Crime, Law and Social Change, 59, No1.

[20] Each ecocide is different and will be subject to evidentiary procedures. Some potential situations that might be prosecuted as ecocide if they occurred at such a time that an ecocide law was in place could be Chevron/Texaco's pollution of the Lagos Agro region in Ecuador, the toxic waste dump of the ship Probe Koala on the Ivory Coast and Shell's pollution of the Niger Delta.

others.[21] What is also stated in the Oslo principles is that no single source of law alone requires states and enterprises to fulfil their principles. These sources are local, national, regional and international and derive from diverse substantive canons, including *inter-alia,* international human rights law, environmental law and tort law. Environmental law has primarily been based on statutory and regulative force, and hasn't yet possessed a strong philosophical or jurisprudential base.[22] It has existed almost delinked from legal history and been forced to rely upon deference to the political question and unnecessarily ended in a web of technical complexity that often supports environmental degradation rather than protect against it. In law, ecocide will not stand-alone and will emerge as environmental law grapples with its proper place as a canon of law with its own rich historical links. What follows is only a few of the important developing bodies of law that support the inclusion of ecocide as an international crime against peace by building upon doctrines that link humanity with the environment as trustees, stewards and equally, potential violators of the duty to protect.

- International environmental crime.

Importantly, a well-established international legal regime exists for environmental crimes (eco-crimes) however its mandate is limited to transboundary harm in relation to the movement of hazardous wastes and illegal fishing, logging and wildlife trade. Penalties

---

21 Mark-Allan Gary, "The international crime of ecocide", *California Western International Law Journal,* Volume 26, Num. 2, pp. 215-271
Mark A. Dumbly, "Waging War Against The World: The Need To Move From War Crimes To Environmental Crimes" 22 *Fordham International Law Journal* (1998), pp. 122 ss.
Mark A. Dumbly, "International Human Rights, International Humanitarian Law, and Environmental Security: Can the International Criminal Court Bridge the Gaps?", *ILSA Journal of International & Comparative Law,* Vol. 6, Issue 2 (Spring 2000), pp. 305-342
Falk, Richard A. (1973): 'Environmental Warfare and Ecocide – Facts, Appraisal, and Proposals'. In: Thee, Marek (ed.), *Bulletin of Peace Proposals.* 1973, Vol. 1. Universitersforlaget, Oslo, Bergen, Tromsö; pp.80–96.
Tomuschat, Christian (1996). 'Crimes Against the Environment'. In: Environmental Policy and Law. 1996. Vol. 26, 6. p.243.

22 The foundations of environmental law differ within different jurisdictions, are unsettled and intersect with state regulation, the tortious duty of care and international treaties

range from imprisonment, the paying of fines to restorative damages. This area of international law has been enacted and extended within many domestic jurisdictions, and despite its narrow mandate and administrative law foundations, the growth of environmental criminal jurisdictions speaks to development of norms prohibiting violence against the environment. However these eco-crimes may occur within weak governance states without the resources to prosecute and, as international eco-crimes currently have a strictly defined frame of reference they often don't cover legalised crimes such as those permitted by state regulation and often perpetrated by transnational corporations, which have resulted in large swathes of territory and eco system destruction.[23] In July 2015 a resolution of the General Assembly of the United Nations explicitly encouraged member states to adopt effective measure to counter crime that impact upon environment and connected the illicit trafficking in wildlife with undermining good governance, the rule of law and threatening national stability which points to an articulation of the importance of ecocide law. While ecocide is part of the family of eco-crimes its proposed status as a *jus cogens* norm means that it is the final threshold of accountability and not yet accounted for in law.

- Human rights

Environmental law is now seeking roots outside the regulatory frameworks of statutory delegation of administrative and planning law into the increasing intersection between

[23] Further support for Ecocide emerged in the recent Resolution of the General Assembly of the United Nations on "Tackling illicit trafficking in wildlife"(30 July 2015) which included: encouraging Member States to adopt effective measures to prevent and counter the serious problem of crimes that have an impact on the environment and recognised that illicit trafficking in wildlife contributes to damage to ecosystems and rural livelihoods (...), undermines good governance and the rule of law and, in some cases, threatens national stability as well as reaffirming the intrinsic value of biological diversity and its various contributions to sustainable development and human well-being, and recognizing that wild fauna and flora and their many beautiful and varied forms an irreplaceable part of the natural systems of the Earth which must be protected for this and the generations to come". Resolution A/RES/69/314 on *Tackling the Illicit Trafficking in Wildlife*

human rights regimes and environmental degradation. Many proponents of ecocide law base their reasoning upon the rich areas of international human rights and environmental law. The influential theory of Vasek's concept of three generations of rights which separated civil and political, economic and social from environmental and collective rights meant that human rights that intersect with environmental conditions were in the third category of emerging rights which includes group and collective rights, right to self-determination, right to economic and social development, right to natural resources, right to communicate and communication rights, right to participate in cultural heritage, right to food, right to life, health human dignity and international equity and sustainability. [24] [1]

The rise of the indivisibility doctrine of international human rights law serves well to make the necessary connection between those human rights traditionally seen as inalienable such as civil and political rights, and their inherent dependence with environmental rights. This doctrine of interpretation allows the linkage between the right to livelihood with the right to life, the right to freedom from persecution with land rights and the right to human health with environmental degradation to become clearer. The indivisibility doctrine extends Vatek's theory beyond his argument of the temporality of rights within a generational emergence, which perhaps resulted in states avoiding the full gambit and interconnected nature of human rights. However what remains is that the bypassing of the third generation of rights, where the human environmental connection is most articulated, is endemic both domestically and in the international law regime. If the indivisibility of human rights doctrine, with all its difficulties of balancing and conflict

[24] Vasak's concept of three generation of rights is useful to examine the emerging rights that are important within these jurisdictions. He proposes that the first generation of rights are the civil and political whose responsibility mainly rests with the state, the second are economic and social right and the third emerge as environmental and collective rights which are the responsibility of states but also affect non-state actors such as transnational corporations. For the purposes of this paper the third generation of rights, and their overlap with the second generation, are what ecocide, eco-crimes and environmental rights elucidate. A recent and precient paper on the crimes against future generations is E. Gaillard, Crimes against Future Generations, Epublico Revist Electronic De Direito Publico, No5, 2015, ISSN 2183-184X accessed at http://e-publica.pt/pdf/artigos/crimes-against-future-generations.pdf

of laws, prevailed in judicial interpretation and legislative action, then the human right to health and right to livelihood could extend into environmental protection. The increased legal proximity between human and environmental rights is being seen in the interpretative method of the European Court of Human Rights (ECtHR) as well as the administration of the African Charter on Human and Peoples Rights (The Banjul Charter).

Significantly, the ECtHR has taken an approach increasingly responsive to shifting social realities in ECHR Member States (an approach often referred to as 'evolutive'), to the scope of guaranteed rights, and which crucially expresses 'growing and legitimate concern both in Europe and internationally about offences against the environment'[25]. The Court has emphasised that effective enjoyment of Convention rights depends on a healthy environment and as environmental concerns have moved up the agenda both internationally and domestically, the Court has increasingly reflected the idea that human rights law and environmental law are mutually reinforcing.[26] It is also highly significant that the ECtHR has shown increasing willingness to draw upon international environmental principles, standards and norms to draw out the human rights implications of environmentally risky actions. The ECtHR is highly responsive to 'evolving convergence as to the standards to be achieved' and has held that it is 'of critical importance that the Convention is interpreted and applied in a manner which renders its rights practical and effective, not theoretical and illusory'.[27]

---

[25] Grant, E, Grear, A, Kerns, T, Morrow K and Short, D. (2014) 'A Human Rights Assessment of Hydraulic Fracturing and Other Unconventional Gas Development in the United Kingdom', Report for the Bianca Jagger Human Rights Foundation. Available at http://extremeenergy.org/2014/10/30/full-report-a-human-rights-assessment-of-hydraulic-fracturing-and-other-unconventional-gas-development-in-the-united-kingdom/
[26] Ibid, 14
[27] Ibid, 15

Admittedly the rights held by humans' amounts to a list as long as the genealogy in the book of Genesis. What many laws lack, but is becoming increasingly articulated, is recognition that the original point of the fulfilment of all rights rests upon the existence of a viable environment. The inalienable dignity of humanity has roots in the earth, therefore environmental degradation and the climate crisis attack the viability of human rights, both legally and literally. In this context contemporary conditions ask for legally binding and enforceable instruments at the international, and not only regional, level to protect them. What the indivisibility doctrine of human rights does, in conjunction with the evolutive interpretative method, is draw seemingly competing rights of civil and political, social and economic into greater proximity and realistic encounter with environmental rights and the duty to protect the environment as a pre-condition of the realisation of human rights.[28]

The right to a healthy environment is not a *jus cogens* norm - yet.[29] If the right to a healthy environment was *jus cogens* then ecocide law stands as a positive enforcement of this right and is a logical and practical extension of the human right to life. The prophetic dissenting judgement of Weeramantry J in the *Danude* case at the International Court of Justice indicates the possible emerging legal reasoning that elucidates ecocide as the prohibitive point of the international norms in human rights, sustainable development and other international treaties.[30] While ecocide is not mentioned in his judgement, the reasoning articulated the emerging jurisprudence outlined in this paper. The very recent Oslo principles also express demands from influential jurists from around the world that law step into its role as adjudicator and interpreter of contemporary realities. This

[28] Currently an International Human rights and Business Treaty is being negotiated at the United Nations that could potentially close some gaps in the accountability and governances relating to the human rights that intersect with the environmental degradation perpetrated by Trans- national corporations. The existence, even of such a proposal, indicates that international law is moving towards pre-emptive steps.
[29] This is despite this right being enshrined in the majority of domestic constitutions. The right to a healthy Environment is rising as a point of concern and investigation by many United Nations agencies including the Human Rights Council and UNEP.
[30] *Gabcikovo-Nagymaros Project (Hungary v Slovakia) (1997) ICJ Rep. 7, 429-555.*

document explicitly outlines specific obligations to be met by states and businesses if climate change and its catastrophic effects are to be averted and implies that critical legal responsibility needs to be taken and can be achieved by a radical movement of the law into obligations and enforcement. This steps into a new era of environmental law: not merely about regulation and statutes, but situated in deep principles of human and environmental rights and obligations. However, at the time of writing, civil claims have consistently failed because the evidentiary requirements for casual connection between the environment and human rights are too tenuous within that jurisdiction. This is where ecocide law would enter as a clear prohibition not solely dependent upon human rights law. In light of the changing human rights culture where the environment is increasingly becoming an explicit part of claims, ecocide law is a reasonable and vital part of this growing legal culture, which would elucidate the indivisibility of human rights, within a criminal framework.

- Public interest, duty of care, fiduciary relationships and the global commons.

Across the globe, within different jurisdictions and with diverse legal mechanisms, a legal movement is growing that proposes a renovation of environmental jurisprudence. This jurisprudence has its basis in environmental law as well as the commons, fiduciary duties, trust and public interest doctrines. Across numerous domestic jurisdictions, from the USA, to India and Holland, cases are being launched in civil and administrative law against governments and statutory authorities to fulfil their duty of care towards those within their jurisdiction, and beyond, and the claims are based upon the protection of the trust and public interest doctrines, tortious claims and an extension of duty of care principles.[31] While outside criminal law's ambit, all of these cases and judgements,

---

31 *Urgenda Foundation* v *The State of the Netherlands (Ministry of Infrastructure and the Environment)* [2015] Case C/09/456689/HA ZA 13-1396 [English Translation].
At the time of writing state appellate courts in the USA have allowed Atmospheric Trust Litigation lawsuits and administrative petitions brought by students to go forward in New Mexico, Texas, Alaska, Oregon,

particularly those from India, point to the growing body of law that express the prohibitive parameters of the harm that can be permitted by state bodies against the environment and confirms a responsibility to protect. This is being witnessed in the atmospheric trust and public interest cases and the rise of tortious claims based upon negligence, nuisance etc.

Ecocide law might seem outside the ambit of these cases, however the work of Mary Woods follows in the footsteps of many legal theorists and scholars who argue that while we exist within the confines of the social contract in law, we are yet to enshrine or enact recognition of what Michel Serres calls the *Natural Contract*, or Woods calls *Natures Trust*.[32] The public trust doctrine compels government, as trustee, to protect natural inheritances such as air and water for all humanity and asserts public property rights to crucial resources. This doctrine is present in numerous jurisdictions across the world, as well as the international community itself. It also doesn't contradict state sovereignty. Rather than being based upon the political discretion of government officials, as a constitutional right these public trust cases express ancient Roman origins in public property rights (res communes) and has roots in European, Asian, African, Islamic and Anglo and indigenous legal cultures.

The jurisprudential void that has existed regarding humanity's responsibilities towards the environment, and the global commons, can be filled by the enforceable enshrining of obligations such as jus cogens norms that are elevated to the level of international crimes.

Colorado and Pennsylvania (Amicus briefs). Petitions on Atmospheric Trust Litigation are pending in the Philippines, the Ukraine, Uganda and Belgium. In Pakistan : http://www.theguardian.com/environment/2015/oct/07/pakistan-high-court-comes-to-defence-of-climate

32 Serres, Michel. *The Natural Contract.* trans. Elizabeth MacArthur and William Paulson. Ann Arbor: The University of Michigan Press, 1995.
Wood, Mary Christina, *Nature's Trust. Environmental Law for a New Ecological* Age, New York, Cambridge University Press, 2014.

Cases that proceed under the public trust doctrine ask for clarification on the positive duty to protect both human citizens and natural environments, and ecocide law enforces these obligations. Thus public interest (natures trust) and ecocide law are complementary as ecocide can be envisioned as not just a breach of a legal duty of care (civil) but the violation of the duty to protect. Transboundary harm and the protection of the global commons are central to the reasoning that elevates ecocide as an international crime against peace.

While awaiting international recognition these issues are being played out in domestic claims with increasing intensity. It is important to recognise that national jurisdictions are often deficient in addressing transboundary or transnational affects without international legal support. Equally, due to the rise in cases and claims based upon arguments of potential or existing transboundary harm, there currently exists both an overburdening of domestic jurisdictions and a void within international law that does not aid the ability of domestic jurisdictions to respond to the acute problems of climate change and ecocide, which are crisis of the global commons. For example, the global commons are generally only protected by soft law instruments; thus the Arctic effectively remains open for exploitation unless political will determines otherwise as the legal restraints are very weak.

The public trust doctrine connects with intergenerational justice and the inter-temporal trusteeship of the planet, which Edith Brown Weiss put forward in 1989.[33] There is a growing body of law that recognises the interests of future generations but, as yet, no binding international legal instrument enforces them. Intergenerational equity has been recognised in the celebrated decisions of the Philippines Supreme Court such as in *Oposa*

[33] E. Brown Weiss, *Our Rights and Obligations to Future Generations for the Environment*, 84 AM. J. INT'L L. 198,200-02 (1990); *see also* E. BROWN WEISS, IN FAIRNESS TO FUTURE GENERATIONS: INTERNATIONAL LAW, COMMON PATRIMONY AND INTERGENERATIONAL EQUITY 25-26 (1989).

v Factoran, J.R[34] where the plaintiff children, representing future generations, were recognised as legal persons. As such they were given legal standing to file the case based on the concept of intergenerational responsibility. Intergeneration rights are articulated in international human rights doctrines so future generations rights have also been considered at the ICJ in the case of Denmark v Norway[35] and the Advisory Opinion on the Legality of the Threat or Use of Nuclear Weapons.[36] Transgenerational rights are complementary to the application of the precautionary principle, which emerged from the Rio Declaration in 1992 and has subsequently become part of judicial reasoning in many jurisdictions. The precautionary principle, which originated in the middle-ages as 'first do no harm', has a weightier significance due to the temporality of climate change and has been enshrined in numerous conventions in international law. Ecocide law protects the interests of future generations by protecting territory from harm. Crimes against future generations, implied within ecocide law, would apply to acts or conduct undertaken in the present which seriously harms the natural environment, human populations, species or ecosystems in the present and has long term consequences.

Across the world there are numerous court cases and emerging (or re-emerging) legal doctrines, within very diverse jurisdictions and based upon very different legal claims, which range from tortious claims against governments for not fulfilling their obligations to cut their emissions quotas to challenging permits for new coal mines to the prevention

[34] Minors Oposa v. Secretary of the Department of the Environment and Natural Resources or Oposa vs. Factoran, *G.R. No. 101083 July 30, 1993*, (S.C., January 1994) (Phil.), 33 I.L.M. 173 (1994)).
Also in *Minors Oposa v. Secretary of the Department of Environment and Natural Resources* (Supreme Court of Philippines, 1993): focused on intergenerational responsibility and justice where it was found that the government had an obligation to preserve the environment and a corresponding "duty to refrain from impairing" it (p.240)

[35] Maritime Delimitation in the Area Between Greenland and Jan Mayen (Den. v. Nor.), 1993 I.C.J. 38, 277 (June 14) (Sep. Op. Weeramantry), *available at* http://www.icj-cij.org/docket/ files/78/6761.pdf.

[36] Advisory Opinion on the Legality of the Threat or Use of Nuclear Weapons, 1996 I.C.J. 226, 243-244 (July 8), *available at* http://www.icj-cij.org/docket/files/95/7495.pdf. The ICJ embraced a broad definition of the environment. It "represents the living space, the quality of life and the very health of human beings, including generations unborn." *Id.* at 241.

or compensation for ecocide. From the smallest administrative land tribunals to national Supreme Courts, citizens and organisations are asking law to move, and what they have in common is a call for recognition of the violence being done to both the earth and the livelihoods of humans and other inhabitants. Each jurisdiction adapts the limit point of harm against ecosystems according to their pre-existing canons and hopefully what will emerge in this process is *a jus cogens* norm of universal jurisdiction owed to all (*erga omnes*) with regards to humanity's intimate and interdependent relationship with the environment and its duty to not violate that obligation. The enshrining of this obligation is the responsibility of international law.

ECOCIDE LAW: THE PROHIBITION AGAINST HARM.

Ecocide law raises the normative value of civil doctrines and human rights that intersect with the environment. Eco-crime is a unifying term that incorporates ecocide, and ecocide law's function as a jus cogens international crime is to mark the final normative threshold beyond which it is illegal to cross. Currently no such threshold exists. Unlike human rights and other areas of criminal law, environmental law presently can be interpreted as possessing a seemingly an opened unanswered legal question without a strong prohibition point or capacity to hold individual perpetrators accountable. It often appears, as seen in the many civil legal cases where *forum non conveniens* has been used as a defence, that perpetrators of environmental destruction are fictive characters without concrete links, or accountability to the damage or territories upon which this destruction is visited.[37]

[37] *Forum non Conveniens* is a common law, conflict of law doctrine - where courts may refuse jurisdiction over matters when there is a more appropriate forum available. Its abuse has been seen most strongly in the famous Chevron/Texaco law suits over the Lago Agrio pollution in Ecuador, which would potentially qualify as an ecocide. Also of interest is the work of the legal realist Felix Cohen and his influential essay "Transcendental nonsense and the functional approach" which is as applicable now for environmental law area as it was once for social realism. Cohen, Felix. Transcendental Nonsense and the Functional Approach, *Columbia Law Review*, Vol.xxxv, June 1935, No 6. Pg 809- 849.

Due to the transboundary nature of ecocide, it is most appropriate that it is enacted at the level of international law subject to the complementarity principle. Ecocide law, as a jus cogens statement, could be sine qua non of all the emerging jurisprudences around environmental law. Essentially, ecocide law would be a strong declarative statement by the international community as to the prohibition of significant human harm to nature and could encompass anthropocentric, biocentric and ecocentric approaches. Ecocide law recognises that law is primarily 'social' regulation, which prohibits significant harm on damage the social body of humans can do to the world in which they inhabit. Criminal law is the most powerful jurisdiction when it comes the regulation and prohibition of harmful activities within the social body due to its enforceability and backing by the state.

As every ecocide is different the courts role is to measure the duration, impact and significance of the evidence before them and this is where judicial reasoning becomes vital.[38] The introduction of ecocide at an enforceable international level also fulfils the normative desire to prohibit, pre-empt and prevent the most grievous of harm vital to any criminal law regime. And as mentioned, it would also protect against corporate crime and crimes against future generations as well as enforce indigenous rights, among many others.

Without criminal law as a counterpart to civil and public interest law that can enforce and penalise the violence enacted against the environment, we are left with a legal war against all: as Hobbes most aptly said *bellum omnium contra omnes.*[39] As science is clearly articulating, to be legitimate states must fulfil the role of sovereign power to protect their

---

[38] Many proposals for ecocide law refer to the 1976 ENMOD which applied to ecocide law this would apply outside warfare and applies a test that does not impose an arbitrary limit, but an analyses of size, duration and impact to be judicially determined.

[39] Ironically the statement rested upon the war being vested in the state of nature. Now we face a war of all against all unless we set limits on the violence against nature, inclusive of humanity.

territory, and others territory, upon which their rule relies. In various civil cases the evolution of state responsibility extending to a duty protect the environment is emerging.[40] In a nutshell, the failure to limit violence on the earth is an abdication of state responsibility, as seen in the public trust doctrine. This results in legal absurdities where it's legal for military and police forces to arrest or even shoot environmental protestors, yet not illegal for individuals to commit extreme violence against eco-systems that human life depends on.[41] Environmental law is on the cusp of stepping into this legal void to negotiate with power, with sovereignty, where it can be recognised that the legal foundations of state power rest upon the viability, inclusive of ecological viability, of the territory under its care and control.

International ecocide law will not solve the world's problems. There is no one legal fix. Ecocide law, however, is an important part of the legal pantheon that can serve to halt massive damage and destruction and give environmental law legal weight, rather than leaving the most serious and dangerous environmental issues to soft consensus, extra-judicial forums or locked into the non - justiciable space between state sovereignties.

ECOCIDE LAW PROCEDURE.

Essentially ecocide law is a both a peacetime and wartime crime and aimed at the prosecution of individuals. Due to the ubiquitous nature of environmental harm, the difficult question of causation arises when it comes to climate change and taking into

[40] *Urgenda Foundation* v *The State of the Netherlands (Ministry of Infrastructure and the Environment)* [2015] Case C/09/456689/HA ZA 13-1396 [English Translation].

[41] One example is Peru's law no. 30151 discussed at http://www.theguardian.com/environment/andes-to-the-amazon/2014/jun/29/peru-licence-to-kill-environmental-protestors accessed 12 October 2015.

account global supply chains as well as what Rob Nixon calls the slow violence of environmental harm[42]. In the pantheon of emerging environmental crimes ecocide law rests with the most serious, most obvious crimes against the environment. This addresses the accountability gap and the lacunae between transnational corporate power as one of the main perpetrators of ecocide, whether as a privatised state entity or as separate. As much environmental damage can be masked by either reliance on regulatory permits, or the labyrinthine and extra legal free trade adjudication process, ecocide seeks to make the corporate and state veil transparent. There will be, like all international legal reform, political and procedural difficulties in introducing ecocide into international law. But how much more violence has to occur before the law recognises that the environmental version of the Holocaust has already appeared on the landscape?

Many commentators on ecocide law agree that strict liability and superior responsibility, as per all international crimes, be part of its elements.[43] Others argue that mens rea is an essential element of the crime following the established norms of the ICC.[44] Many argue

[42] Nixon, Rob. *Slow Violence and the Environmentalism of the Poor*, London, Harvard University Press, 2011. This book also implies that ecocide law is linked to alleviation of poverty

[43]There has been much discussion and disagreement over the strict liability proposals for ecocide law. Some argue that is important for the effectiveness of the ecocide provision to capture not only the actus reus standard of criminal law, but also negligence, reasonable foreseeability, wilful blindness, carelessness and objective certainty standards which animate tort and civil liability. This reflects a long legal tradition, certainly in the UK of not requiring mens rea for certain types of offences especially pollution offences. See also international: HNS Convention 1996 (International Convention on Liability and Compensation for Damage in Connection with the Carriage of Hazardous and Noxious Substances by Sea). The effectiveness of ecocide law is that it is free of the restrictions of criminal intent. Features that can highlight why an ecocide event occurs such as neglect, wilful blindness to risk or indeed intent, do not determine the commission of the offence but play pivotal role in the determination of the sentence. Whilst some suggest some form of mental element be included as part of the offence itself, by confining recklessness or intent as a factor in sentencing has a practical application; it is an aggravating feature. What is central to a pollution/hazardous/significant harm event is not so much why it occurred, but its factual impact.

[44] These arguments rest upon the refusal of a definition by the states without the condition of mens rea. Also these arguments point to ecocide being one of the most serious of crimes which not all ecocrimes are. The international law of the most serious crimes is exceptional, with specific rules (prosecution, prescription), and should be limited to a short list of actions against the environment. To counter this Neyret proposes an expansive definition of "intention"as the environmental criminality is specific and different than crimes against human dignity. The differences over whether mens rea should be included

that the adjudicating forum needs to be empowered to decide on both criminal and civil matters. Consistent with the liberal notion that criminal punishment should be a last resort, criminalising harm to the environment could incorporate alternate, non-penal means as has been proposed by many ecocide law commentators such as Higgins.[45] It has been proposed that the remedies for ecocide, with other challenges such as climate change, shall also be based upon restorative justice and compensatory elements.[46] This could be enacted within the criminal arena to reflect in the principles of state common but differentiated responsibilities, which is expanding within international law. Whether this is addressed within the current purview of the Rome Statute by the appointment of a separate prosecutor or administered by a separate UN body is a question to be decided.[47] Currently the ICC doesn't have much room for restitution, injunctive powers, the ability to determine civil liability or to clean up the harm. This introduces the well-formed argument for a separate international convention for ecocide and the environment administered by its own secretariat and enforced by its own court. However, part of the issue with all international law is that, with the exception of free trade agreements, enforcement and regulation remains a problem.

CONCLUSION.

The introduction of ecocide law would confirm the emerging environmental legal norms summarised above. In conjunction with civil and soft law movements', ecocide law announces to companies and states that responsibility and legal consequences flow from

---

also springs from different juridical histories and definitions of mens rea. http://papers.ssrn.com/sol3/papers.cfm?abstract_id=1940084

45 Higgins, Polly, *Eradicating Ecocide*, London, Shepeard- Walwyn Ltd, 2010.

46 The entry point for international criminal law is imprisonment. If Ecocide Law is a strict liability crime this lowers the entry point thereby allowing alternative sentencing to be included.

47 There are also proposals for a separate United Nations Trusteeship to administer environmental assistance according to the mitigation, adaption and restoration needs of the affected communities and territories.

serious violence and damage of eco-systems. [48] The viability of ecocide being inserted into the Rome Statute, or alternatively being the impetus for an alternative forum such as an International Environment Court, is universally considered difficult at the present time, but there are numerous legal and political reasons why these hurdles need to be overcome. Civil society, jurists, scientists, United Nations agencies, individual citizens and nation states cognisant of the environmental degradation of their territories combine to express a groundswell of support for the urgent creation of a normative threshold regarding environmental violence. In this context, ecocide law is a legal necessity that surpasses considerations of political lethargy.

Ecocide law at the international level, or even the simplest gesture of declaring at a UN assembly that ecocide is an international crime, would address the accountability and governance gaps in current international environment law. Additionally it would send a message to Trans-National Corporate actors that certain activities will be too risky to undertake due to the potential penalties. While it may take awhile for the jurisprudence on ecocide, and more broadly environmental harm, both within the civil and criminal jurisdictions, to develop more nuanced coherent language, ecocide brings to the table the legal prohibitions. It is a legal urgency and asks law to regain its rightful and reasonable role. In light of science and civil society demands, ecocide law is a moral and legal imperative upon which much, including human and environmental livelihoods, depends.

---

[48] Across the world NGOs, governments and citizens are embarking in legal action in both defensive and affirmative claims to halt environmental damage. These immense legal efforts can be assisted and fast tracked by an international statement that ecocide is a jus cogens crime.

ABRIDGEMENT AND CONFERRAL OF JURIDICAL PERSONALITY

Gary Lilienthal[+]

Senior Lecturer, School of Law

College of Government and International Studies

Universiti Utara Malaysia

Nehaluddin Ahmad[*]

Professor, Department of Law

Sultan Sharif Ali Islamic University (UNISSA)

Brunei Darussalam

Key words: Juridical personality, meta-law, epideictic rhetoric, tropes, artefact, slavery.

Abstract

The significance of this paper is in its identification of a supra-legislative process, *a priori* to the legal system, delivered as rhetorical dialectic among great state orators. The paper's objective is to examine this rhetorical process, to see how it might be constituted and superadded to the legal system's recognition of juridical personality. Juridical personality is important in domestic law as well as in international law, because it indicates who has access to the legal system. This article is structured to pose the question as to how this meta-system of law might be superadded onto the legal system. The article's argument tries to prove that such a meta-law consists of a special kind of public oratorical rhetoric, comprised of special arrangements of rhetorical tropes

[+] LL.B., (Sydney University, Australia), Grad. Dip. Legal Pract., (College of Law, Sydney), M.Psychoanalytic Studs., (Deakin University, Australia), Ph.D., (Curtin University, Australia). Email: gary@uum.edu.my; garylilienthal@gmail.com

[*] MA, LL.B., LL.M. (Lucknow University, India), LL.M. (Strathclyde University, UK), LL.D. (Meerut University, India). Email: nehaluddin@unissa.edu.bn; ahmadnehal@yahoo.com

embedded in epideictic rhetoric. The paper's methodology arises from the dialectic discourse between Bentham and Hart, in which laws were considered to be artefacts of the human will. The article will suggest that with a natural devolution of juridical personality to the most reasoning and legally competent persons always in operation, the sovereign could simply alter it, by application of epideictic rhetoric. This could control the cohort of juridical personalities in the sovereign's sole interests.

Introduction

The significance of this paper is in its identification of a supra-national legislative process, *a priori* to the legal system, contrived as rhetorical dialectic among great state orators, to the sometime detriment of members of society. This dialectic operates on people's juridical personalities,[1] namely, their ability to engage in the legal system and seek its remedies. The paper is even the more significant, as it deals with transnational legislative rhetoric beyond the control of the subject populations. Further, it revives a moribund field of scholarly rhetorical theory, formerly taught widely in the schools as epideictic oratory, but now used mainly at the transnational level. Also, the paper conducts a critical theoretical analysis of juridical personality, a concept masked by the apparent quality of the legal system. While society lauds the intelligence and subtlety of itse legal system as its mode of dispute resolution, it ignores discussion of whether the system is accessible.

The paper's objective is to critically examine this rhetorical process, to see how it might be structured. The concepts in this article are not new. Rather, their currency has fallen out of the education system, even although the state uses these techniques to great effect, to this day. This discussion tries to revive the importance of these hidden instruments of governance, to explain their effect on rights and the courts' jurisprudence.

[1] See B Smith, 'Legal Personality' (1928) 37(3) *The Yale Law Journal* 283, 283.

Juridical personality is important in domestic law as well as in international law. It interacts with the meta-legal system of international law. Its operation could be observed in Germany's mass manufacture of concentration camp corpses, which came after the historically and politically intelligible preparation of what Arendt called the living corpses.[2] It was intelligible because it followed a plain logic of necessary and catastrophic movements. First was the destruction of the juridical person.[3] Then came the murder of the moral person.[4] Finally came the destruction of unique identity, the spontaneity through which a person might still call an action "mine".[5] It was a necessary and catastrophic process of reducing human persons to animal slavery, and this article investigates the necessity in that process. Only that human destruction beginning with obliteration of the juridical and moral personality could create this kind of systemic significance.

It was a three-part process of destruction. Annihilation of the juridical personality required the deprivation of all civil and political rights. It made some categories of person outside the law's protection, through denationalization, and consequently making individuals into outlaws. This meant that the concentration camp inmates were nonagents. They had no capacity for civil or criminal legal action. Mostly, these individuals were innocent. They were jailed only for who they were. Murder of the moral persons required incapacitation of their consciences' operation. For this, the concentration camps made death anonymous. This robbed death of its natural meaning as the conclusion of the fulfilled life.[6] This destruction of individuality began with the removal of all distinguishing characteristics, it continued by sadistic torture, and proceeded with systematic ruin of human bodies. It was calculated to destroy everyone's

[2] H Arendt, *The Origins of Totalitarianism*, (Meridian, 1958) 447.
[3] Ibid 447.
[4] Ibid 451.
[5] Ibid 453.
[6] Ibid 452.

human dignity.[7] More than six million human beings died in Germany during NAZI times, but no one could ascertain how many juridical persons perished first.

Arendt's analysis shows catastrophic and irresistible movements against the interests of the people. Apparently, they were powerless to resist this process of regulation against human character, where people were punished and destroyed merely for acting according to their natural characters. Therefore, this article proposes to critically investigate the rhetoric associated with those catastrophic changes, referred to above. Argument is structured to pose the question as to how this apparently *a priori* system of law might be superadded onto the legal system. Since it is *a priori* to domestic law, and to an extent, extrinsic to the legal and legislative systems, a better term for it would be "meta-law",[8] for purposes of this paper's discussion. Therefore, this article's argument tries to prove that such a meta-law consists of a special kind of public oratorical rhetoric, comprised of special arrangements of rhetorical tropes. Directly relevant to this context, Quintilian called a trope the conversion of a word or phrase, from a proper sense to another kind of signification, noting that tropes were deployed in order to increase greatly a word or phrase's force or power.[9]

The paper's methodology arises from dialectic discourse between words of Bentham and words of Hart. Bentham's view was that laws were only either commands, prohibitions, or, permissions. Only as such, they were artefacts of the human will.[10] For Bentham,

[7] Ibid 454.

[8] The term "meta-law" means outside, but essential to, the practice of law. Meta-legal would mean something in the ethical domain *a priori* to law, but affecting and circumscribing court doctrines. It is likely that meta-legal process subsists in the public mind as an unconscious process.

[9] Quintilian, *Institutes of Oratory*, VIII. 6. 1.

[10] Artefact. Something observed in a scientific investigation, or experiment, that is not naturally present, but occurs as a result of the preparative or investigative procedure. *Oxford English Dictionary*, 2nd edn, (Clarendon Press, 1989).

such artefacts excluded the subsistence of the natural law,[11] based as it was on natural kinship relations. However Hart rebutted this by noting that legislators must still be guided by natural and rational precepts, and they must use these natural laws with reason to critique the current law.[12] Thus, arguably, there is dialectic discourse between those who say law is merely commands, prohibitions or permissions, and those who say legal reasoning must be guided by natural law and reason. It is from this dialectic that the artefacts of the human will might arise. They may be unintended consequences of a rhetorical process. They might arise due to the rhetorical constriction of legal reasoning to mere commands, prohibitions or permissions. Thus, this article proposes an investigation into the kind of tropes giving rise to those catastrophic changes, as referred to above.

Argument begins with an introduction to the 2008 Australian High Court case law on slavery, as it apparently ignored grievances associated with the plaintiff's status. Then follows an examination of Gorgias' *Encomium to Helen*,[13] to see how epideictic rhetoric could veil catastrophic meta-law within publicly-acceptable procedural systems. Discussion follows through the arguments of later rhetorical scholars, to show how a rhetorical device might be used to trigger inevitable and necessary catastrophic shifts, beyond the resistance consequent on public cognisance. Argument proceeds by applying these well established, but rarely considered, rhetorical ideas to the legal doctrines surrounding juridical personality and slavery. This step is essential because juridical personality seems to be subject to court doctrine - taken and given apparently capriciously at any time, with serious and possibly unintended consequences. An examination of the nature of juridical personality will require a prior brief consideration of the nature of rights, duties, privileges and their correlates. This is based on the

[11] Jeremy Bentham, *The Collected Works of Jeremy Bentham* (Oxford University Press, 1990), "Of Laws in General" 26

[12] H L A Hart, 'Bentham and the Demystification of the Law' (1973) 36(1) *The Modern Law Review* 2, 4.

[13] D M MacDowell, (ed), *Gorgias, Encomium of Helen* (Bristol Classic Press, 2005).

premise, discussed above, that the destruction of juridical personality is necessarily *a priori* to the systematic annihilation of rights.

The article will suggest that, with a natural devolution of juridical personality to the most reasoning and legally competent persons always in operation, the sovereign could simply alter the effluxion of this devolution, by application of epideictic rhetoric. For example, same-sex marriage, presented as the trope of "marriage equality", conferred juridical personality on a cohort of people by altering this sovereign process. This could control the group of juridical personalities, in the sovereign's sole interests. It tends to sustain the view that meta-law is an artefact of sovereign artifice, to control access to the courts, in the sovereign's sole interests.

Slavery

As discussed above, slavery is the end point of annihilating the juridical personality. In the 2008 Australian High Court case of *R v Tang*,[14] the High Court upheld Mr Tang's slavery conviction, based on a breach of the criminal statutory provision,[15] but declined to take on board the more expansive understanding of the 'powers attaching to the right of ownership' that the Australian Human Rights and Equal Opportunity Commission (HREOC) had put forward. The HREOC, as intervener, constructed its view of the law on slavery based heavily on the *Kunarac Case*.[16] It identified a non-exhaustive list of the 13

[14] (2008) 237 CLR 1. Mr Tang had operated a Melbourne brothel and was convicted of slavery.

[15] Slavery has been a criminal offence in Australia since the Imperial Slave Trade Act of 1824. In 1999, the Commonwealth of Australia Government inserted a collection of slavery offences into division 270 of the Criminal Code Act 1995 (Cth). Section 270.1 of the Criminal Code defines the term 'slavery' as "the condition of a person over whom any or all of the powers attaching to the right of ownership are exercised, including where such a condition results from a debt or contract made by the person". It is an offence under section 270.3(1) to: possess a slave, or exercise over a slave any of the other powers attaching to the right of ownership; engage in slave trading; enter into any commercial transaction involving a slave; or exercise control or direction over, or provide finance for, any act of slave trading or any commercial transaction involving a slave. *Criminal Code 1995* (Australia), div 270.

[16] *Prosecutor v Kunarac,* Case No. IT-96-23 (22 February 2001).

indicia of slavery that would infer a power attaching to a right of ownership had been exercised. At the head of that list was the partial or total destruction of the juridical personality of the victim.[17] However, since slavery was said to have been unknown to the English common law,[18] people with the status of a slave, or *de facto* slaves, could not benefit from manumission.[19] In this way, their de facto status of slavery was irremediable at common law.

The International Court for the Former Yugoslavia (ICTY) had heard some forced labour cases under the heading of enslavement. Enslavement came under Article 5(c) of the Statute of the Tribunal.[20] Forced labour also might be charged as a violation of the laws or customs of war under Article 3 or as a form of persecution pursuant to Article 5(h).[21] The ICTY carried out a detailed analysis of the required elements of enslavement in *Prosecutor v Kunarac*.[22] The facts of that case were grounded on various acts of sexual abuse. The Court elaborated a definition of enslavement in *Kunarac*, then applied it in the forced labour case of *Krnojelac*.[23]

In *Kunarac*, the defendants were charged with enslavement for, among other things, detaining two girls in a house for many months and treating them as their personal

17 Amicus Curiae Brief, *R v Tang* (High Court of Australia) (HREOC, Submission in Support for Leave to Intervene and Submissions on the Appeal , 5 May 2008)
18 W Blackstone, *Blackstone's Commentaries Vol, III* (William Young Birch, 1883) 79.
19 Although there is evidence that villeins could be manumitted. Blackstone, above 18, 95, 97, 400.
20 *Statute of the International Tribunal for the Prosecution of Persons Responsible for Serious Violations of International Humanitarian Law Committed in the Territory of the Former Yugoslavia since 1991*, U.N. Doc. S/25704 at 36, annex (1993) and S/25704/Add.1 (1993), adopted by Security Council on 25 May 1993, U.N. Doc. S/RES/827 (1993).
21 Article 5 deals generally with 'crimes against humanity'. Both 'enslavement' and 'persecution' are listed there. Article 3 deals with violations of the laws and customs of war. Slavery has been held to be a violation of customary international law. See Krnojelac Trial Judgment paras. 352-353.
22 *Prosecutor v Kunarac,* Case No. IT-96-23 (22 February 2001).
23 *Prosecutor v Kunarac,* Case No. IT-96-23 (22 February 2001) and Case No. IT-96-23-A (12 June 2002) (Appeals Chamber); International Labour Office, 'Casebook of Court Decisions', 2009, p. 19.

property. The girls had to do all the housework and comply with all the defendants' sexual requirements.[24]

The question before the Trial Chamber was what was meant by enslavement as a crime against humanity under Article 5(c). The Trial Chamber reviewed the applicable laws. These included the Slavery Conventions,[25] the Forced Labour Convention,[26] the Nuremberg Charter,[27] decisions of the European Court of Human Rights,[28] including *Van der Mussele*,[29] and the works of the United Nations International Law Commission.[30] The Trial Chamber held that enslavement was a crime in customary international law, which consisted of the exercise of any, or all, of the powers ascribing to the right of ownership over a person,[31] for which property might be considered as a trope. The Trial Chamber decided that enslavement incorporated elements of forced labour and stated several factors as relevant.[32]

The Appeals Chamber confirmed the chief thesis of the Trial Chamber that the customary concept of slavery, which was defined in the 1926 Slavery Convention and referred to as chattel slavery, had developed further to include various new forms of

[24] International Labour Office, *Casebook of Court Decisions* (International Labour Office, 2009) 19.

[25] *Slavery, Servitude, Forced Labour and Similar Institutions and Practices Convention of 1926*.

[26] *Convention concerning Forced or Compulsory Labour* (Entry into force: 01 May 1932).

[27] *Charter of the International Military Tribunal – Annex to the Agreement for the prosecution and punishment of the major war criminals of the European Axis*, 1945.

[28] See European Court of Human Rights, *Guide On Article 4 Of The Convention Prohibition Of Slavery And Forced Labour* (European Court of Human Rights, 2014).

[29] *Van der Mussele v Belgium* - 8919/80 [1983] ECHR 13 (23 November 1983).

[30] See the *Statute of the International Law Commission* 1947.

[31] *Kunarac Trial Judgment* para 539.

[32] Elements of control and ownership: the restriction or control of an individual's autonomy, freedom of choice or freedom of movement; the accruing of some gain to the perpetrator. The consent or free will of the victim is absent. It is often rendered impossible or irrelevant by, for example: the threat or use of force or other forms of coercion; the fear of violence, deception or false promises; the abuse of power; the victim's position of vulnerability; detention or captivity; psychological oppression or socio-economic conditions. Further indications of enslavement include: exploitation; the exaction of forced or compulsory labour or service, often without remuneration and often, though not necessarily, involving physical hardship, sex, prostitution and human trafficking. International Labour Office, *Casebook of Court Decisions* (International Labour Office, 2009) 20.

slavery. Each of these was also based on the exercise of any or all of the powers attaching to the right of ownership, where a right is nothing more than a claim. This claim might be enforced in the court if the court were to ascribe sufficient juridical personality to the claimant. The Appeals Chamber held that in all cases, as a result of the exercise of any or all of the powers attaching to the right of ownership, there was certain destruction of the juridical personality. This destruction was greater in chattel slavery, but the differences were only of degree. The Appeals Chamber held that these new forms of slavery formed a part of enslavement as a Crime Against Humanity under the customary international law.[33]

The High Court of Australia ignored the argument based in international case law, slavery being unknown to the English common law. It only existed for the Court as a statutory crime. The differential status issues appeared to be non-justiciable. The fact that slavery existed exposed a paradox in the Court's methodology. Slavery must be partially non-justiciable, by virtue of the Courts' omitting to cognise people of abridged juridical personality. This failure of cognition arguably suggests an elision in the court's jurisdiction. The next section examines this kind of elision and some of its consequences.

A Priori or Meta-Law

Around the world, governments have been locking up enslaved victims of human trafficking as if they were the perpetrators of that heinous international crime.[34] The irony demands explanation. They could secure express public consent for this merely on the basis of the trope "turn back the boats". Arguably, this was at once catastrophic in its consequences, and at once ironic, while innocent people were either turned back into the

[33] *Kunarac Appeals Judgment* at para. 117.
[34] S Hoffman, '*Fear, insecurity, & risk: Refugee journeys from Iraq to Australia*', Doctoral dissertation, 2010, Retrieved 20 November 2014 <http://researchrepository.murdoch.edu.au/445 9/>.

wild seas, or jailed without judicial hearing for an indefinite time. It was a mass making of jailed innocent prey, without the victims' ability to move the court to exercise the public power in their interests. They were people with abridged juridical personality. Juridical personality is that unique form of personality known only to the law. Juridical means symbolic,[35] and Smith argued that society could confer juridical personality.[36] It is unclear how society could be moved to do this, or whether it was true.

Sometimes, juridical personality coincides with real human personality. Sometimes it does not. It is of central concern in international law because of the differential status of personalities in the laws of states, citizens and others. International instruments are reduced routinely to municipal law, using due and proper process. The resultant regulations are no doubt lawful. This process has its genesis in great kings speaking to each other, in the public domain, on matters of positioning by arms, with great power of oratorical voice. Such international instruments are thus the language of kings and queens as between themselves, and, therefore arguably within the field of the *jus cogens* in international law.[37] This could be illustrated as follows. The nature of the civilian procedure in the English Court of Chivalry arose in the 1631 case of *Rea v Ramsay*,[38] in which the Court of Chivalry convened to award a trial by duel. However, later the King stopped the fight. Foreshadowing a civilian procedure, Chief Justice Fineux was said to have told King Henry VIII that the jurisdiction of the Court of Chivalry belonged to the law of arms and war between kings, and therefore not to the law of England.[39] This suggests that sovereign international discourse cannot be justiciable in municipal courts.

[35] KF von Savigny, *Das Recht des Besitzes: Eine civilistische Abhandlung* (Gerold, 1865) 206.
[36] Smith, above 1, 283.
[37] A peremptory norm is also called *ius cogens*. It is Latin for "compelling law", and is a fundamental principle of international law. A *ius cogens* norm is accepted by the international community of states, and from which no derogation is allowed. States generally agree that *ius cogens* includes the prohibition of genocide, maritime piracy, all forms of slavery, torture, non-refoulement and wars of aggression and territorial aggrandisement. M C Bassiouni, 'International Crimes: *Jus Cogens* and *Obligatio Erga Omnes*' (1996) 59(4) *Law and Contemporary Problems* 63, 68.
[38] *Cobbett's Complete Collection of State Trials, Vol III*, (Hansard, 1809) 483.
[39] Ibid 483n.

It is a jurisdictional elision, as municipal courts are unable to adjudicate matters of parties to international wars.

Many catastrophic laws have their narrative genesis in the *jus cogens* of international law. By way of illustration, emanating from the China warring states period, the *Lüxing* chapter of the *Shangshu*,[40] dating from no later than the fourth century BCE, reported that Chi You created social disorder. This disorder spread throughout other lands to otherwise peaceful people, and thus, their kings had to learn how to control it. The barbarian Miao people were the first to respond to these international conditions. They controlled it before anyone else, by ignoring virtue and resorting to restraining people with cruel punishments. They created what they called the five oppressive penalties, and just called them the law. This simple effect of the calling of something the law arising from a purely rhetorical act, was thus *a priori* to law. In consequence of a mere process of naming, and in the face of outside public threats of disorder, they killed and slaughtered the innocent, excessively chopped off body parts, severed ears, conducted beatings and branding. The people's juridical personality was abridged by a rhetorical act of the state's rulers.

The *Lüxing* chapter went on to say, by way of hymnal oratory, that the "god-on-high" took pity on the innocent people and created terror to put an end to the oppressive rulers,[41] inferring some kind of external invasion. This suggested an ethical maneuvre of some superadded sovereign power, somehow veiled by hymnal oratory from ordinary public perception. The next section discusses a basis of this kind of rhetorical maneuvre.

---

40 书经， Marquis Lü on Punishments, chapt 55.

41 M Puett, 'Sages, Ministers, and Rebels: Narratives from Early China Concerning the Initial Creation of the State' (1998) 58(2) *Harvard Journal of Asiatic Studies* 425, 436-438.

The Encomium of Helen

Rhetorical oratory delivers the three outcomes of pre-legal ethical deliberation: admonishment, exhortation and rebuke.[42] This section investigates the foundations of rhetorical meta-laws, by reviewing their appearance in the time of the sophist Gorgias,[43] during the axial age.[44] Gorgias made quite a lot of money in his work of instructing wealthy people of high status, in the arts of wisdom, by means of public debates and private instruction.[45] This indicated his instruction had perceived high value to the ruling classes, from which it might be inferred that his instruction was useful in ruling. The *Encomium of Helen* was his rhetorical exercise, apparently designed for didactic purposes.[46] It was the language of inherent excellences, different from hymn[47] and epainos[48] because an epainos was brief, but an encomium was developed artistically.[49] Thus, Gorgias' method was one of artifice.

In *The Encomium to Helen*, Helen was the most notorious woman of Greece. She abandoned her husband Menelaus to run away with Paris, Prince of Troy. The encomium explained it was wrong to apportion blame to Helen. After epitomising her

[42] Aristotle, *The Nichomachean Ethics* (Harvard University Press, 1999), 67.

[43] GB Kerferd, *The Sophistic Movement* (Cambridge University Press, 1999) 45.

[44] "The most extraordinary events are concentrated in this period. Confucius and Lao-tse were living in China, all the schools of Chinese philosophy came into being, including those of Mo-ti, Chuang-tse, Lieh-tsu and a host of others; India produced the Upanishads and Buddha and, like China, ran the whole gamut of philosophical possibilities down to skepticism, to materialism , sophism and nihilism; in Iran Zarathustra taught a challenging view of the world as a struggle between good and evil; in Palestine the prophets made their appearance, from Elijah, by way of Isaiah and Jeremiah to Deutero-Isaiah; Greece witnessed the appearance of Homer, of the Philosophers—Parmenides, Heraclitus and Plato—of the tragedians, Thucydides and Archimedes. Everything implied by these names developed during these few centuries almost simultaneously in China, India, and the West, without any one of these regions knowing of the others." K Jaspers, *The Origin and Goal of History* (Yale University Press, 1953) part I, chapt 1.

[45] Kerferd, above 43, 26.

[46] Ibid 30.

[47] Hymn. A book, film, or other composition praising someone or something. Oxford English Dictionary, above 10.

[48] Epainos means praise. The Oxford Classical Dictionary, (Clarendon Press, 2012) 505.

[49] GA Kennedy, *Progymnasmata – Greek Textbooks of Prose Composition and Rhetoric* (Society of Biblical Literature, 2003) 108.

birth and her marriage, it suggested four possible causes for why she went to Troy. They were: (a) mere chance by virtue of the gods; (b) excess of force; (c) persuasive oratory; or, (d) the exigencies of love. Each of these was overpowering and irresistible. If she were subjected to any of them, she would be blameless. Rather than praise Helen, the encomium defended her from criticism. Gorgias demonstrated that speech was too powerful a sovereign. It could either arouse or assuage fear, sorrow, pity or joy.[50] His method suggested such overwhelming force, that the audience could only agree Helen was a mere pawn in the events of her life.

However, the *Encomium to Helen* pursued a schema of truth. Its stated purpose was to use speech for constructing the truth. It advised against any action based on either contingent facts or opinion,[51] because speech could have the same bodily effect as drugs. Action followed inevitably and necessarily from belief. With a mastery of the art of rhetoric, the speaker could compel people to do anything he wanted.[52]
The encomium demonstrated that persuasion could be veiled as mere instruction or a demonstration to professionals of oratorical skill. Gorgias could captivate the learned, using their own professional discourses,[53] thereby minimising opposition to his veiled message. Their professional discourses gave him access to their systems of command, which he could interweave into his apparent truth.

The question arises as to how Gorgias could ground his rhetoric, sufficient to move the will of the audience physically, as might a law physically move an audience either to remove or confer juridical personality.

---

50 Gorgias, above 13, 12.
51 Ibid 14.
52 Ibid 15.
53 Ibid 15.

Gorgias' Epideictic Style

This section critically examines the techniques of Gorgias. Rhetoricians agreed that there were only three kinds of rhetoric. The first was the deliberative, about public affairs, or in general to persuade someone to do something or accept a point of view. Deliberative rhetoric would have a topic of either expediency or inexpediency, by means of exhortation or dehortation. Forensic rhetoric was where someone sought to defend or condemn someone's action. It had a subject of justice or injustice and was by means of accusation or defence. Epideictic rhetoric was also known as demonstrative, declamatory, panegyrical or ceremonial. It was the most ornate kind of oratory, concerned primarily with the present.[54] It tended to shade into the other two types. Orators used epideictic rhetoric for the particular topics of honour and dishonour, achieved by means of praise and blame.[55] With these bases, the epideictic style could be used for either denunciation or promotion, or even the kind of "terror" calculated to put an end to oppressive rulers, as discussed above. It achieved these ends by dealing with virtues and vices, personal assets and achievements.[56]

A partial list of pairs of virtues and vices was: courage and cowardice; temperance and indulgence; justice and injustice; liberality and selfishness; prudence and rashness; gentleness and brutality; loyalty and disloyalty.[57] Other assets and achievements could be used. Examples could be physical attributes, external circumstances such as family background, education, economic status, political, social and religious affiliations, and friends; achievements, such as work achieved, services rendered, honours won, offices

[54] E P J Corbett and R J Connors, *Classical Rhetoric for the Modern Student* 4th edn, (Oxford University Press, 1999) 23, 24.
[55] Ibid 24.
[56] Ibid 127.
[57] Ibid 128.

held, wise sayings and testimonials.[58] Epideictic rhetoric could thus be deployed to confer differential status, separating out those of such a status that they ought to be punished. It could be seen as the rhetoric of the ruler, because it suggested an inherent authority to confer or withdraw status. Those deploying epideictic rhetoric ornamented their oratory with references to the higher attributes, without requiring any reference to facts. Therefore, an artefact could arise where the epideictic rhetoric conflicted with the facts while being entirely plausible. This suggested conversion of a word, or phrase, from a proper sense to another kind of signification.

Epideictic rhetoric presented itself as a mere verbal artifice, an apparent contrivance of utterance in whatever discourse used, such as within the lawyers' or the physicians' discourses.[59] Considering it as the rhetor's contrived display of skill, the epideictic rhetor naturally demonstrated his skill before a learned audience, who alone felt qualified to assess his skill. The epideictic rhetor might advocate any position, however frivolous or however serious, just as long as he could parade his rhetorical skills.[60] He could hide his work behind a veil of skill demonstration. An example might be a King's discourse designed to demonstrate regal character while veiling a new policy announcement. The audience would enjoy the regal speech for its regalness, and not cognise its artefact of a new command policy.

The Gorgian rhetoric did not show existing things to the audience and did not need to ground its argument in the facts.[61] Because many underlying discourses might subsist, it opposed dogmatic adherence to one single discourse as the sole path to constructing the truth. Instead, it construed what was accepted as rational and transparent, underlying its efforts for persuasion. This allowed the rhetor to relate the presented virtues to whatever

---

58 Ibid 129.
59 S Consigny, 'Gorgias's Use of the Epideictic' (1992) 25(3) *Philosophy & Rhetoric* 281.
60 Ibid 281.
61 Ibid 287.

discourses people already accepted and used. [62] The rhetor might confer status, or lack of it, or even withdraw it, in an acceptable way to the audience, through the recognized protocols of a particular discourse being spoken.[63] For example, the rhetor proposing same-sex marriage would simply utter the human rights trope "marriage equality", conferring the status of marriage on same-sex couples. With an understanding of the various professional discourses, their rules and their protocols, the orator could ignore reality and persuade the most learned, by reference to the discourse of their own cultus.[64] With a masterful display of the cultic procedural rules, the epideictic rhetor could veil the force of any inferred command within apparent audience agreement.

In consequence of this, Gorgias could offer an ornamented epideictic oration, purporting to admonish the audience with relevant facets of honor and virtue, appealing to the propriety of the audience cultus without reference to facts, but veiling direct commands to them. Arguably, these commands would be artefacts of the epideictic methodology, and would precipitate action, which evidenced meta-law. Later, when the audience realised that they had been moved beyond their cognizance, and without their express consent, this would amount to a catastrophic manipulation of the human will by an external human will.

The next section considers these artefacts of epideictic methodology, to see how sovereign commands could be transmitted into the mass audience.

[62] Ibid 288.

[63] Corbett, above 54, 51. But consider the concept of cultus as apotropaic use of magical thinking to institutionalise a ritual perpetuation of the past, relying on public memory to ground deception by artifice, based on the lures of persuasive rhetoric.

[64] Cultus means the routinized ritual process, evidenced in public loyalty, representing certain inner principles and meanings, performed publicly without reference to those inner meanings.

Necessary, Inevitable and Catastrophic

Rhetoric was the art of using language either to persuade or to influence others. It was the body of rules a speaker or writer had to follow for expression with maximal eloquence. This meant rhetoric was, on the one hand, the ability to create an event, and, on the other hand, a mandatory code requiring obedience.[65]

A rhetorical discourse had power to cause events. As examples, it could produce events of persuasion, of understanding, or of revelation. Rhetorical analysts attempted to account for these discourse events by identifying structures, patterns and figures constituting the rhetoric. However, there was a problematic and discontinuous relationship between the structures of tropes and the persuasion of rhetoric.[66] Description of the structure was inadequate to explain the cause of an event. The analyst could not ascertain which particular events a discourse had generated. Thus, rhetoric must have been a composite discourse of structure and event.[67] This suggested that the perception of any event inferred the prior and completed operation of some operative rhetorical structure, beyond the human consciousness.[68]

---

[65] J Culler, 'On Trope and Persuasion' (1978) 9(3) *New Literary History* 607, 608.

[66] See below for a full discussion of tropes, where a trope will be described as the conversion of a word or phrase, from a proper sense to another kind of signification.

[67] Culler, above 65, 608.

[68] A suitable place to examine that fundamental part of the rhetoric called tropes, would be with Quintilian in his seminal work on rhetoric, *The Institutes of Oratory*. Quintilian called a trope the conversion of a word or phrase, from a proper sense of another kind of signification. This would be to increase the word or phrase's force. Quintilian, above 9, VIII. 6. 1. He categorized those tropes, which were most important and most frequently in use. In this categorization, he stated that the purpose of some was for adding to significance, and for others, merely for ornament. Some tropes were within words used correctly, and others were in words used metaphorically. Tropes could occur in single words, in thoughts, or inside the very structure of the composition. Quintilian, above 9, VIII. 6. 2. In the tropes used for adding to or amending significance, there might also be embellishment. However, some were intended only for decoration. Quintilian, above 9, VIII. 6. 3. The most common trope was metaphor. (A figure of speech in which a word or phrase is applied to an object or action to which it is not literally applicable: "when we speak of gene maps and gene mapping, we use a cartographic metaphor". Oxford English Dictionary, above 10.) Even the illiterate used it unconsciously. However, when used, it would always be apparent. Quintilian, above 9, VIII. 6. 4. It increased the profusion of the language by borrowing what the language

Kellner argued that, within rhetoric, there was an apparent absence of any identified nexus between superficial sentence structures and the innate fabric of the text, suggesting veiled transmission of information. This included the thought structure underlying the work[69] and suggested the text might subsist in the unconscious. However, tropes, in particular, had developed recognised and natural transforming powers, causing a rapid expansion in the field of rhetorical critique. This new cognition of trope-based critical strategies arose from the master tropes schema of renaissance rhetoric.[70] These were metaphor, metonymy, synecdoche, and irony. This four-trope system allowed so many ways of prioritizing the human experience that it deserved detailed attention.[71]

The four-trope series had a natural movement through a stable course. It was a natural series in a state of flux. There was movement from metaphor, as an *a priori* naming phase, to metonymy, the process of formalization within a cultus. Then there was a movement to the integrative synecdoche, where the audience assimilated the communicated information. Then there was a final audience awakening that all of these four methods were turns relative to each other, in sequence, and that the whole process

did not have. In doing this, a noun or a verb might be transferred from a place in the language where it belonged. Alternatively, it might go to another location where there was either no correct word or where the metaphorical word was better than the proper form. Quintilian, above 9, VIII. 6. 5. Where this transference lacked necessity, added significance, or ornamentation, the transference would be vicious. Quintilian, above 9, VIII. 6. 6. Arguably, such transference could confer reduced juridical status, as discussed below. The trope synecdoche (A figure of speech in which a part is made to represent the whole or vice versa, as in England lost by six wickets (meaning ' the English cricket team'). Oxford English Dictionary, above 10.) gave variety additional to metaphor in language, by understanding plural from singular, whole from part, genus from species, following from preceding and the reverse. Quintilian, above 9, VIII. 6. 19. The trope of metonymy (The substitution of the name of an attribute or adjunct for that of the thing meant, for example suit for business executive, or the turf for horse racing. Oxford English Dictionary, above 10.) was not so different to synecdoche as it was the substituting of one word for another. It indicated an invention by the inventor or something possessed by the possessor. Quintilian, above 9, VIII. 6. 23. Thus, custom permitted oratory to signify what was contained from what contained it. For example, consider: "well-mannered cities"; "a cup was drunk"; and "a happy age", Quintilian, above 9, VIII. 6. 24, or even a rights-bearing foetus.

[69] H Kellner, 'The Inflatable Trope as Narrative Theory: Structure or Allegory?' (1981) 11(1) *Diacritics* 14, 14.

[70] Ibid 15; and see below for D'Angelo's explanation of the genesis of the four master tropes.

[71] Ibid 16.

had been ironic.[72] The entire process having been ironic, irony necessarily inferred prior and completed operation of the four-trope series.

The preceding suggests the tropes were the system by which the mind conceived the world through language. These four master tropes represented a sequential program with natural forces of propulsion. Thus, Vossius' statement was incorrect that the order of the tropes, as was conventional to thinkers among 17th-century rhetoricians, was due to their frequency of appearance.[73] It was this precise order of the four-trope system that was effective to exploit the mind's innate propensity for understanding by narrative structure.[74]

These successive changes seemed unrestrained, catastrophically abrupt, and their movements apparently discontinuous. This inferred an automatic, unconscious activity of the mind.[75] Catastrophic trope movement might be the primary indicium of the force of public persuasion, such as public acceptance of ironic policy outcomes. People might well be persuaded by this meta-law that a human being was not a juridical person.

Vico was one of the first arguing for four primary tropes, from which all the figures arose.[76] Vico had considered these tropes as representing the stages of consciousness on its automatic road to abstractness.[77] The tropes described relationships between phenomena in the experiential world.[78] The four master tropes were a movement from global, through analytic, then through synthetic processes. In this contextual frame, metaphor was holistic, metonymy dispersive, synecdoche integrative, and irony was

[72] Ibid.
[73] G-J Vossius, 'Rhetorique de l'ironie' (1978) 30 *Poétique* 495, 497.
[74] Kellner, above 69, 17.
[75] Ibid 28.
[76] FJ D'Angelo, 'Prolegomena to a Rhetoric of Tropes' (1987) 6(1) *Rhetoric Review* 32, 32.
[77] G Vico, *The New Science* 3rd edn, (Cornell University Press, 1970) 85-91.
[78] D'Angelo, above 76, 33, 34.

reflective.[79] It suggested that an orator might make a general statement, a metaphor, and the audience themselves might consequently and necessarily synthesise an ironic outcome by reflection.

It was relevant to this proposition of over-determined audience response that,[80] in her study of the psychology of metaphor, Gertrude Buck[81] regarded metaphor as the necessary stage, through which speech must pass to arrive at literalism. She had concluded that only via the metaphor might abstract ideas manifest into existence as an abstract statement of fact.[82] Metaphor was identifiable as a necessary precondition to law, the creation of fact from ideas, and therefore was meta-law.

An epideictic orator could begin the process of government by speaking a powerful metaphor, based in honour and virtue, framed in the public cultus. A trope would always increase the power of the oratory. This metaphor might react with the population at unconscious levels, not entirely cognised until during the stages of synecdoche and metonymy. The public mind would turn, tropicly, through catastrophic shifts of reason, modelled by the four master tropes. This rotation would construct new meaning in the public mind. It would resonate in the public mind, by attribution, simulated and false phenomenological properties, which would feel like real events. The public would reflect then perceive these rhetorical events as facts. This oratory would stimulate the usual real bodily responses to those events, by signalling the bodies' senses. At last, the people might speak of a certain irony, in that outcomes were inconsistent with initial suggestions and expectations. However, by this time, the oratory would have controlled the audience's bodies, beyond their cognisance, as if by the orator's personal ownership. Irony would always signal that the 4-trope series was at the point of completion, and the

[79] Ibid 34, 35.
[80] Ibid 39.
[81] G Buck, *The Metaphor: A Study in the Psychology of Rhetoric* (Inland Press, 1976) 43.
[82] Ibid.

orator would have exercised, merely by the meta-law within oration, a catastrophic power of ownership over physical human bodies. The signal of irony is arguably an artefact of metaphor used within epideictic discourse.

This suggested the possibility of people accruing duties, without express agreement, and without accruing correlated rights, via some application of meta-law. Possibly, these duties were just called "non-legal", but were strictly enforced administratively. The next section considers the nature of the relationship between rights and duties, to see what effect on it epideictic rhetoric might have.

Rights, liabilities, duties, privileges and liberties

Just as the relationship between a word and its meaning is arbitrary,[83] there has been a continuing tendency to confuse legal and non-legal ideas. Often, there was a catastrophic swing from one to the other. Some ideas were arbitrarily designated as "non-legal". Not only lay persons, but also judges sometimes tended to confuse legal and non-legal ideas. Also, an uttered term could blend these two senses, conveying uncertain meaning.[84] This section investigates the Correlativity Axiom of Hohfeld and shows how it failed, whenever epideictic rhetoric was directed at the issue. This fundamental axiom was that every right correlated with a duty. Stated another way, the existence of a right necessarily entailed the existence of a duty, and vice versa.[85] Duties without rights, coinciding in the same person, would be suggestive of enslavement.

---

[83] Bally & Sechehaye, (eds), *Course in General Linguistics – Ferdinand de Saussure* (McGraw-Hill, 1966), 127, 128.
[84] W N Hohfeld, 'Some Fundamental Legal Conceptions as Applied in Judicial Reasoning' (1913) 23(1) *The Yale Law Journal* 16, 21, 22.
[85] J E Penner, 'The Analysis of Rights' (1997) 10 *Ratio Juris* 300, 300.

Rights were illustrated in the 1895 case of *Wilson v Ward Lumber Co.*,[86] in which the court held that the commonly used meaning of the term "property" signified any external object over which someone exercised the right of property. Thus, property was metonymy, indicating that the mention of property meant effluxion of the four-trope series had already begun. This wide term included every kind of acquisition, over which a man might own or maintain an interest.[87] Professor Jeremiah Smith, when he was Mr. Justice Smith, stated in *Eaton v B. C. & M. R. R. Co.*[88] that, strictly, land was not property, but rather, the subject of property. The term "property" meant only the owner's rights in relation to it. It signified a right over a particular thing. Property was any person's right to possess, enjoy, use, and dispose of a thing.

Because fundamental legal relations were *sui generis*, attempts at definition would fail.[89] Hohfeld argued this problem away by saying it was better to describe the various relationships from a tabulation of opposites and correlatives, as follows. Jural opposites were: rights and no-rights; privilege and duty; power and disability; immunity and liability. Jural Correlatives were: right and duty; privilege and no-right; power and liability; immunity and disability.[90] There has been a sustained critique of Hohfeld's schema, including the proposition that all eight concepts could be reduced to right and

86 (1895) 67 Fed. Rep., 674, 677.
87 (1895) 67 Fed. Rep., 674, 677.
88 1651 NH, 504, 511.
89 For Bentham, definition *per genus et differentiam* (An Aristotelian pattern of definition that proceeded by citing a genus to which a term belonged, and then the difference that gave its species and so located it within the genus. The classic example was the definition of humans as rational animals. *Oxford Reference*, <http://www.oxfordreference.com/view/10.1093/oi/authority.20110803100317283>, retrieved 20 April 2015), was the proper and preferred form of definition,[89] and no other would suffice. Considering the legal fictions of right, obligation or power, the logician could find no genus of any of them. This meant definitions of legal fictive terms must be by some alternate process, necessarily not definition *per genus et differentiam*. Bentham suggested that a class of fictitious entities would be identified, and then the lawyer could merely associate the right, or other fiction, to this class.[89] The association could be deceitful and lend itself to denunciation or false aggrandisement. In this way, a right was not a species of anything, but a right had many species distinguishable by means of the benefits which each conferred. CK Ogden, *Bentham's Theory of Fictions*, reprint from the original 1932 edition, (Routledge, 2002) lxxvi, lxxviii.
90 Hohfeld, above 84, 30.

duty.[91] Also, there was an old doctrine of *damnum absque injuria*, appearing to make Hohfeld's axiom far less axiomatic. The doctrine of *damnum absque injuria* explained that some acts causing an aggrieved plaintiff would carry no remedy.[92]

Consider that A's right against B that B should stay off A's land correlated with B's duty toward A to remain off the land. The term "right" was synonymous with the word "claim". Thus, Lord Watson stated in *Studd v Cook*[93] that "Any words which in a settlement of moveables would be recognized by the law of Scotland as sufficient to create a right or claim in favor of an executor . . . must receive effect if used with

[91] A Halpin, *Rights and Law: Analysis and Theory* (Hart Publishing, 1999) 27-48.

[92] Weeks' 1879 treatise proposed that the doctrine of *damnum absque injuria* might be understood as follows. A tort was a civil wrong for which compensation in damages was recoverable. This was in contradistinction to a crime, which was punished by the criminal law system in the interest of society-at-large. Every invasion of a legal right, such as the right of property, or the rights incident to the possession of property or the right of personal security, constituted a tort. So also may an injury to the person, character or reputation of another, constituted a tort. In order to constitute a tort, two things must occur: actual or legal damage to the plaintiff; and, a wrongful act committed by the defendant. In as much as a tort implied damage coupled with a wrongful act, *damnum absque injuria* was damage without a wrongful act, as the law understood the term. The literal definition of the term *damnum absque injuria* was damage without injury. However, it was difficult to conceive of a damage done without a corresponding remedy to the party alleging itself to have been damaged. Thus, enlarging the above definition, still confined to the definitions of Latin transliterators, the term might be better explained as damage, loss, harm, injury, or hurt without wrong or injustice. *Damnum*, in the civil law, was the diminution of a person's property and was either *factum*, already done, or *infectum*, apprehended or threatened. The former might arise from either mere accident or free will of another. The latter might have arisen during the exercise of a right enjoyed by the person causing it. In either case no reparation had to be made for causing it unless it was done wrongfully. In that case, the person injured was entitled to compensation. *Injuria*, in the civil law, was a broad term signifying every action contrary to law. In a specific sense, it meant the same as *contumelia*, outrage. Strictly speaking, *injuria* was a wrongful act or tort that related to the defendant, and *damnum* was the loss sustained, or harm done, by an injury, and related to the plaintiff. The injury done must be a violation of a right to which the plaintiff was entitled. Also, the plaintiff must suffer legal damages from it. Damage was defined as the loss caused by one person to another or to his property either with the design of injuring him or with negligence and carelessness or by inevitable accident. He who had caused the damage was bound to repair it, and if done with malice, might be compelled to pay beyond the actual loss. If damage was caused by accident without anyone's blame, the loss must be borne by the owner of the thing injured. However, there were certain acts done, accidents and casualties occurring, by which there was a lawful use of one's own property occasioning lossess to others. For such acts, the law afforded no remedy and they were designated as *damnum absque injuria*. EP Weeks, *The Doctrine of Damnum Absque Injuria considered in its relation to the Law of Torts* (Sumner Whitney & Co, 1879) 2, 4, 6, 7, 7n, 8.

[93] (1883) 8 AC 577.

reference to lands in Scotland."[94] This meant that wordage recognised by the legal cultus as creating a right of property in moveables for an executor would create a similar right of property over land. The context was hypothetical, and the implied command was based in the rules of the audience's professional discourse. It was epideictic rhetoric using a meta-law to command a new right.

Consider the proposition that a privilege was the opposite of a duty. It correlated to a "no-right." When A had a right or claim that B must stay off A's land, A had the privilege of entering the land. This was equivalent to saying that A had no duty to stay off the land. This meant a privilege to enter negatived the duty to stay off it. However, if A contracted with B for A to go onto A's land, then A had, in respect of B, both the privilege and duty of entering the land,[95] the metaphoric word "contract" being a legal construction and term of art, suggesting that contract signalled epideictic rhetoric.

Lord Lindley stated in *Quinn v Leathem*[96] as follows.

> The plaintiff had the ordinary rights of the British subject. He was at liberty to earn his living in his own way, provided he did not violate some special law prohibiting him from so doing, and provided he did not infringe the rights of other people. This liberty involved the liberty to deal with other persons who were willing to deal with him. This liberty is a right recognized by law; its correlative is the general duty of every one not to prevent the free exercise of this liberty except so far as his own liberty of action may justify him in so doing. But a person's liberty or right to deal with others is nugatory unless they are at liberty to deal with him if they choose to do so. Any interference with their liberty to deal with him affects him.[97]

---

[94] Ibid 597.
[95] Hohfeld, above 84, 32.
[96] (1901) AC 495.
[97] Ibid 534; Hohfeld, above 84, 36.

However, in this passage was a sudden shift, apparently a *petitio principii*, in the use of terms. First, the "liberty" in question was changed into a "right". Then, possibly because of juxtaposition to the word "right", the reader might assume that the correlative must be "the general duty of every one not to prevent . . . ."[98] Nevertheless, the passage simply exemplified ironic outcome in the judge's use of the word "liberty". It began with the seemingly irrelevant metaphoric reference to the status of the British subject.

In Mackeldey's Roman Law,[99] the author explained that positive laws contained either general principles from the rules of law or for special reasons, they established something differing from those principles. In the former case, they carried a common law, in the latter a special law. The latter would be either favorable or unfavorable to people's rights as it enlarged or restricted the common rule. The favorable special law and the right it created in the Roman law were termed by the tropes "the benefit of the law" or, "privilege".[100] Thus, the English word "privilege" was commonly used to mean a particular legal advantage belonging to some individual or class of people. There were judicial opinions[101] recognizing this meaning.[102] From this, the dominant technical meaning of the word "privilege" was the negation of the legal duty.[103] The best synonym of legal "privilege" would be legal "liberty".[104] Thus, a duty could be negated with the epideictic "special" law.

There were instances of standalone duties, such as criminal law duties, public law duties. Examples would be a duty to pay taxes, a duty imposed by regulators, and, duties to

[98] Hohfeld, above 84, 37.
[99] F Mackeldey, *Handbook of the Roman Law*, Volumes 1-2 (T and J W Johnson, 1883) 164.
[100] The same view is taken, but less explicitly, in Rudolph Sohm, *Sohm's Institutes of Roman Law* 2nd edn, (Oxford University Press, 1901) 28.
[101] *Smith v Floyd* (1893), 140 N. Y., 337, 342; *Lonas v State* (1871). 3 Heisk, 287, 306, 307; *Territory v Stokes* (1881), 2 N. M., 161, 169, 170; *Ripley v Knight* (1878), 123 Mass., 515, 519; *Dike v State* (1888), 38 Minn., 366; *Re Miller* (1893), 1 QB 327.
[102] Hohfeld, above 84, 38.
[103] Ibid 39.
[104] Ibid 42.

plants, animals, or inanimate objects.[105] These appeared to breach the correlation axiom, because they were duties direct to the sovereign, where the sovereign was the source of meta-law.

It was possible that Hohfeld directed his analysis only to private law, excluding the public and criminal laws. Private and public law duties to the dead did not correlate with a right.[106] The ostensibly *sui generis* rights to treat people, animals and inanimate objects in particular ways were liberties, which correlated with no-rights.[107] Since they were not rights, their actuality failed to refute Hohfeld's correlativity axiom, stated above.[108]

Under undisturbed common law, an individual acquired legal personality upon live birth. Thus, a foetus did not have legal rights. According to the correlativity axiom, therefore, no one owed a duty of care to a foetus. Thus, substandard conduct that injured a foetus could not be a breach of duty to that foetus. Prenatal injuries were irrecoverable. When courts ultimately allowed recovery for injuries sustained in utero, first by viable and then by nonviable fetuses, they usually did so through an extension of legal personhood. To determine this personhood, they followed the latest biomedical knowledge, arguably epideictic, without needing to challenge the correlative axiom. The most critical stage in the expansion of pre-birth legal protection concerned preconception misconduct. Allowing recovery for harm caused by such conduct invalidated the correlativity axiom.[109] One could not argue that preconception conduct breached a duty that correlated with the victim's right, because prior to conception the victim could have no rights. Nonetheless, as observed by Justice White, "an increasing number of courts have

[105] R Perry, 'Correlativity', (2009) 28(6) *Law and Philosophy* 537, 581, 582.
[106] Ibid 581.
[107] A R White, *Rights* (Oxford University Press, 1984) 64, presenting Hart's view that duties imposed by criminal law are not correlative with rights.
[108] Perry, above 105, 581.
[109] Ibid 582.

recognized a right to recover even for prenatal injuries caused by torts committed prior to conception",[110] and they have done so in various settings.

The confluence of the defendant's acts or omissions and foreseeability of harm to a future and unconceived child determined a duty of care. This appeared to get around the correlativity axiom. This kind of duty of care was a separate duty because the unconceived foetus was not a person capable of acquiring legal rights. This suggested the duty of care was an abstract duty, uncorrelated to any right.[111]

Hohfeld's Correlativity Axiom appears to break down easily according to the rules stated in Mackeldey's Roman Law.[112] The relationship between rights and duties appears to be arbitrary. A special law indicates a rule that will break down the axiom. From the examples, above, the process of breaking down the axiom appears to be the deployment of epideictic rhetoric, to make special laws from applying a metaphor as meta-law. As special laws disturb and overturn the common law, they suggest irony as a signal of a prior use of epideictic rhetoric. When the Axiom breaks down, people may incur duties without any correlated rights, the limiting point to which is slavery.

Three Legal Persons and Their Interests

Having suggested meta-law was a trope process, turning through inevitable catastrophic shifts, this section seeks to categorise the various descriptions of juridical personality. It seeks this in order to verify whether or not these categories themselves were tropic. If they were indeed tropic, the reader would expect they might behave like the meta-law. Representing these schools, Naffine posited three legal persons, Juridical Personality

[110] *UAW v Johnson Controls, Inc.*, 499 U.S. 187, 213 (1991) (White, J., concurring).
[111] Perry, above 105, 583.
[112] Mackeldey, above 99, 164.

Type A, Juridical Personality Type B and Juridical Personality Type C. Type A theorists disagreed that the legal personality must build on the metaphysical person. Type B scholars assumed that humanity was the genesis of moral and legal claims grounding legal personality. Type C scholars regarded metaphysical persons as the basis of legal personality.[113]

In Type A, legal personality was nothing more than the formal capacity, or ability, to carry a legal right, and therefore, to participate in legal relations.[114] On this basis, foetuses might be regarded as persons, their rights coalescing at birth.[115] These contingent rights of the foetus were recognised in the Australian case of *Watt v Rama*.[116] Type A did not necessarily carry any status.

The Type B definition was of any reasonable being. It came closest to the ordinary language meaning and was the accepted formal legal definition of person as an animate being.[117] Someone became a legal person in this sense upon birth, as legally defined, and ceased being a legal person upon entire brain death, also legally defined.[118] Status inhering in Type B was due to the person's stage of life.

The responsible subject Type C departed from ordinary meanings of the word "person". Like Type A, it was a technical legal term, with a meaning wholly interior to law. Not all human beings qualified for the status of a Type C person. Only the rational, and thus, the legally competent sat within Type C. Full legal personality of this kind required an

---

113 N Naffine, 'Who Are Law's Persons? From Cheshire Cats to Responsible Subjects' (2003) 66(3) *The Modern Law Review*, 346, 350.
114 Ibid.
115 J Seymour, *Childbirth and the Law* (Oxford University Press, 2000).
116 [1972] VR 353.
117 Naffine, above 113, 353.
118 A Heldrich and A F Steiner, 'Legal Personality' in M A Glendon (ed), *International Encyclopaedia of Comparative Law Vol 4: Persons and Family* (J C B Mohr, 1995) 3, 4.

ability to initiate court actions, or to be sued.[119] This legally and mentally competent adult human was the essential holder of rights.[120] As the typical subject of rights and duties, Type C was the normal human being acting in a unitary capacity, in his or her own right.[121] In Type C, there was the classic contractor,[122] personally accountable for civil and criminal actions, possessing the entire scope of legal rights and responsibilities. Type C conformed to the theoretical construction, applicable in the criminal law, that a human being was a rational creature. He or she was free to choose his or her acts and deserved punishment whenever choosing to act immorally.[123]

Thus the legal system preferred the status of Type C, over Type B, and in turn, over Type C. Any movement in preference and status from Type A to Type B to Type C entailed a progressive exclusion of human beings from the special status of person, steadily reducing the size of the community of legally competent persons.[124] Change from Type A to Type B imposed a requirement for a particular human form. It had to be integrated and complete, self-functioning and individuated from the mother. This movement from Type A to Type B must exclude the unconceived, those foetuses not surviving birth,[125] animals, and the deceased. This symbolic movement also raised questions about the fullness of personality of the pregnant woman. The movement to Type C imposed additional requirements of cognitive individuation, with Type B adding biological limitations, and Type C adding intellectual and moral definitional

---

119 R Tur, 'The "Person" in Law' in A Peacocke and G Gillett (eds), *Persons and Personality: A Contemporary Inquiry* (Basil Blackwell, 1987) 119.
120 M H Kramer, 'Do Animals and Dead People Have Legal Rights?' (2001) 14(1) *Canadian Journal of Law and Jurisprudence* 29, 36.
121 Smith, above 1, 287.
122 A concise description of the contractor of the classical period is to be found in B Coote, 'The Essence of Contract' (1988) 1 *Journal of Contract Law* 183. P S Atiyah has most fully documented the waxing and waning of this classical contractor in P S Atiyah, *The Rise and Fall of Freedom of Contract* (Clarendon Press, 1979). Atiyah has observed nevertheless that the idea that contract law enforces 'the private autonomy of contracting parties' is still with us. P S Atiyah, *Essays on Contract* (Clarendon Press, 1986) 11.
123 L Waller and C R Williams, *Criminal Law Text and Cases* 8th edn, (Butterworths, 2001) 258.
124 Naffine, above 113, 366.
125 Ibid 365.

restrictions.[126] Natural recognition of differential status implied a necessary and inevitable movement from Type A to Type B to Type C, thereby automatically and inevitably removing people's juridical personalities, and their rights. This shift, cognate to the catastrophic shifts in the four-trope series, would limit the cohort of juridical persons to the most rational and legally competent, all others suffering the irony of a realisation of slavery without their express consent.

Within this cohort of juridically competent persons, to be a legally competent person was to be the subject of rights and duties. To confer legal rights or to impose legal duties, therefore, was to confer legal personality.[127] If a society coerced a person to act or forbear in favor of a second person, the latter had the right, and the former owed the duty.[128] Thus, this predictability of social coercion shaped rights and duties. Rights and duties generated the legal personality. Both Salmond and Holland stated their most satisfactory definition of legal personality as capacity for legal relations.[129] However, the word "capacity" suggested an instance where the subject had the capacity for legal relations, without being a party to them. For example, a minor with a capacity to marry might not be necessarily married. However, if society conferred legal personality, then the minor was made a party to legal relations.[130]

Legal personality should be described either as an abstraction predicating legal relations or as a mere name for the precondition to being party to legal relations. However, Gray thought there could be no right, and, therefore, no consequent legal personality, without

---

126 Ibid 366.

127 J C Gray, *The Nature and Sources Of The Law* 2d edn, (Columbia University Press, 1921) 27; J W Salmond, *Jurisprudence: Or The Theory of the Law* 5th edn, (Stevens and Haynes, 1916) 272; T E Holland, *The Elements of Jurisprudence* 9th edn, (West, 1900) 88; F Pollock, *A First Book Of Jurisprudence* (Burt Franklin, 1923) 114.

128 A L Corbin, 'Legal Analysis and Terminology' (1919) 29(2) *Yale Law Journal* 163, 163; A L Corbin, 'Jural Relations and Their Classification' (1921) 30(3) *Yale Law Journal* 226, 226.; O W Holmes, *The Common Law: The Collected Works of Justice Holmes* (University of Chicago Press, 1881), 167 et seq.

129 Salmond, above 127, 88, 91.

130 Smith, above 1, 283.

the will to exercise that right.[131] Despite the premise that a will was necessarily *a priori* to a right, Gray explained with great irony how some human beings without a will, and inanimate objects, had legal personality.[132] Salmond rejoined that no being was capable of rights without being capable of interests susceptible to the acts of others. No being was capable of duties unless also capable of acts affecting the interests of others.[133] However, the same attribution of the right also attributed the corresponding interest. He defined a legal person as any being to whom the law attributed the capacity of interests and consequent rights, and of acts and consequent duties.

As long as the sovereign had unlimited power of attribution to safeguard its interests, neither theory hindered its giving legal personality to anything or anyone.[134] For example, the sovereign could, by oratory, attribute reason to an unreasoning person. This sustained the view that meta-law was an artefact of sovereign artifice in the sovereign's sole interests, with these sovereign interests tending to minimise the community of juridical persons.

Conclusion

The High Court of Australia's decision in *R v Tang* exposed a paradox in the Court's reasoning. By this reasoning, slavery must be only partially justiciable, by virtue of the Courts' elision in cognising people of abridged juridical personality. This elision is catastrophic. Many catastrophic laws have their narrative genesis in the *jus cogens* of international law, and the *Lüxing* chapter was just one example of such a process. It suggested the natural outcome of abridging people' juridical personality would be an ethical maneuvre of some invasive sovereign power.

131 Gray, above 127, 25, 26.
132 Ibid 28.
133 Salmond, above 127, 273.
134 Smith, above 1, 284.

Such a maneuvre could be seen in Gorgias's encomium, demonstrating that persuasion could be veiled as mere instruction, or as a mere presentation to professionals of oratorical skill. Gorgias could captivate the learned, using their own professional discourses, thereby minimising opposition to his veiled message. Arguably, these commands would be artefacts of Gorgias's epideictic methodology, and would precipitate audience action, which evidenced meta-law. Later, when the audience realised that they had been moved beyond their cognisance, and without their express consent, this would amount to a catastrophic manipulation of the human will by an external human will.

An epideictic orator could begin the process of government by speaking a powerful metaphor, based in honour and virtue, framed within the recognised public cultus. This metaphor might react with the population at unconscious levels. The public mind would turn, tropicly, through catastrophic shifts of reason. This rotation would construct new meaning in the public mind, feeling to them like real events, and upon due reflection, perceived as real facts. Therefore, this oratory would stimulate real bodily responses to those events, by signalling the bodies' senses. Irony would always signal that the 4-trope series was at the point of completion, and the orator would have exercised, merely by the meta-law within oration, a catastrophic power of ownership over physical human bodies. The signal of irony is arguably an artefact of the use of metaphor within epideictic discourse. In this way, people could accrue additional duties, without express agreement, and without accruing correlated rights.

Hohfeld's Correlativity Axiom appeared to break down easily according to the rules stated in Mackeldey's Roman Law, rendering the relationship between rights and duties as arbitrary. A special law disturbing the common law indicated a rule that would break down the Axiom. This process of breaking down the Axiom could be achieved with epideictic rhetoric. When the Axiom broke down, people could incur duties without any correlated rights, the limiting point to which was slavery. This inferred that a breakdown in Hohfeld's Axiom would be signalled as the irony of involuntary slavery, such as, for example, with the jailing of victims of human trafficking.

In this way, differential status implied a necessary and inevitable movement from P1 to P2 to P3 personalities, thereby automatically and inevitably removing people's juridical personalities, and their rights. This shift, analogous to the catastrophic shifts in the four-trope series, would limit the cohort of juridical persons to the most rational and legally competent, all others suffering the irony of reduction to slavery without express consent. This sequence arguably operates all the time.

With a natural devolution of juridical personality to the most reasoning and legally competent persons always in operation, the sovereign could simply alter its course, by application of epideictic rhetoric. For example, same-sex marriage presented as the trope of "marriage equality" confers juridical personality on a cohort of people, by altering the Type A-Type B-Type C process. This could control the cohort of juridical personalities in the sovereign's sole interests. It sustains the view that meta-law is an artefact of sovereign artifice, to control access to the courts, merely by an epideictic act of attribution, in the sovereign's sole interests.

A Historical Analysis of the Development of Free Speech Justifications

Twana A. Hassan*

Abstract

Humans are born free in the moral sense. This widely recognized principle of natural freedom implies that exercising freedom should not require moral justification; but rather; its restriction must be based on valid justifications. Nevertheless, the burden of justification appears to have been reversed in the context of free speech. A rich jurisprudence has been developed for justifying free speech. Why and how did such reversion happen? This paper is a historical analysis for answering that question through three arguments. (1) It argues that the primitive forms of mythologies, superstitions and religions can be considered the oldest sources of limitation on expressive activities. (2) It finds that the first restrictive laws of freedom of speech were religious in nature, and the first justificatory arguments for freedom of speech were reactions to such religious restrictions. (3) It concludes that justifications of freedom of expression have evolved in parallel with the manifestation of power in both religious and political institutions. These three critical arguments can be a strong base for asking whether exercising or restricting freedom of speech requires moral justifications.

Keywords: Free Speech, Justifications of Free Speech, History of Free Speech, Development of Freedom of Expression, Limit of Free Speech

---

* PhD Candidate, TC Beirne School of Law, the University of Queensland; Research Scholar, the Center of Public, International and Comparative Law. (twana.hassan@uq.net.au). I am very grateful to Professor Suri Ratnapala for his invaluable and thoughtful comments on the earlier draft of this paper.

I. INTRODUCTION

Humans are born free in the moral sense.[1] The recognition of this natural freedom is found in many religions, ancient writings and philosophical works. It is also widely recognized and accepted as an aspirational provision of international treaties. The first article of the Universal Declaration of human Rights reflects the universal recognition of natural freedom. It reads 'All human beings are born free and equal in dignity and rights.' More importantly, it has been adopted in many legal systems. In many countries, persons are legally treated as free citizens from birth. For example, it is observed that 'the presumption of freedom' has become an embedded principle of the Common Law.[2] The core notion of the principle is that humans are free to do, say, have, and to be whatever they want if there is no law explicitly prohibiting it. In other words, the general rule of human action is that everything is allowed unless it is restricted by a legal rule. An application of that principle is that human freedom does not require justification, but its restriction needs to be justified.

If this is a principal rule regarding freedom, how have philosophers, scholars and thinkers shifted the burden of justification from laws restricting freedom to the exercise of freedom itself, how have they shifted justification from lawmakers to freedom holders? More specifically, how did the exercise of the FoE become burdened with the need for justification? Did not the scholars realize that those who exercise FoE do not need to justify anything, but rather, those who restrict FoE must justify the restriction?

---

1 It can be argued that if this is a statement of fact it is not correct because some people are born in a form of slavery or in cultural and legal conditions that are hard to describe as states of freedom. This potential challenge is a valid legal argument. Nevertheless, my argument for natural freedom is based on moral foundation, namely what ought to be, not on legal reality of the world as it is.

2 See Douglas N. Husak, 'The Presumption of Freedom' (1983) 17(3) *Noûs* 345 A major dimension of the presumption of freedom is the principle of legality whose core notion is that the fate, scope, limit and protection of freedoms and fundamental rights must not be solely and unconditionally left to the judicial interpretations and ambiguous legislative words. For further explanations on this principle, see Dan Meagher, 'The common law principle of legality in the age of rights' (2011) 35(2) *Melbourne University Law Review* 449

Surprisingly, without a serious consideration of these fundamental questions, scholars have produced a rich jurisprudence of FoE justifications. Many theories, doctrines and approaches have been initiated and developed to morally or legally justify the exercise of FoE.[3] How have these justifications of FoE been developed? This is the central question for most of the arguments and perspectives presented throughout this paper. Its main purpose is to provide a historical analysis of the development of FoE justifications. The analysis is obviously a major undertaking. It requires a comprehensive examination of the origin of many values, interests, norms, rights, and other considerations that play a central role in both justifications and limitations of FoE. The concept of power seems to provide a theoretical framework for examining those values and considerations altogether. Therefore, what follows is an examination of the impact of the emergence of various forms of power on the development of FoE justifications.

II. POWER AND EXPRESSIVE ACTIVITIES IN PRIMITIVE COMMUNITIES

My starting assumption is that to understand the historical foundation of justificatory theories of FoE, one may need to investigate the origin of power and its nature because throughout human history power has been a major, if not the only, reason behind whatever that has happened to all forms of freedom, including FoE. In this paper, power is used in the sense of directing, influencing, restricting or controlling the free will of others. The emergence of various forms or institutions of power has played a significant role in conceptualizing all forms of freedom including FoE. Apparently the emergence of power has ultimately forced the defenders of freedom to initiate and develop justificatory arguments for FoE against different forms and various manifestations of power.

[3] See Larry Alexander, *Freedom of speech* (Ashgate, 2000)

There is no evidence suggesting that there were customary restrictive rules on expressive activities, or there was an idea of FoE justification in ancient times, especially before the emergence of institutionalized religions and political power. No one had to justify expressive activities due to the absence of power in early human communities. This statement can be supported by both 17th and 18th centuries' political theories of the state of nature and evolutionary anthropology.

For most of theories based on the state of nature life and freedom are twins born together on earth. Humans started living on earth freely.[4] They were born with whatever potentials and capacities required for being a free agent. Being free and remaining so was a characteristic of humans in early forms of life. In his Second Treatise of Government, John Locke powerfully describes the state of nature, before the emergence of political institutions, as the state of 'perfect freedom,' and 'equality.' He writes 'To understand political power right, and derive it from its original, we must consider, what state all men are naturally in, and that is, a state of perfect freedom to order their actions.'[5]

Anthropological evidence concerning the earliest human communities also does not suggest that humans' expressive activities were dependent on providing justification to any form of power. The history of freedom can be reasonably extended as far as we can trace the beginning of human life on earth. Whenever and wherever there was a human being, there was freedom in a sense. To deny that, one must first deny the existence of humanity and the existence of free will as an integral part of humans. The earliest known humans and indeed their hominid ancestors lived in rudimentary societies or family groups or tribes. These groups were bound together by customary rules. The freedom of

[4] How can it be proved? This is a difficult question. It is as challenging as asking how it can be disproved.

[5] John Locke, *The second treatise of government: (An essay concerning the true original, extent and end of civil government), A letter concerning toleration* (Blackwell, 1966)

group members to do as they please was limited by these rules. There is no evidence suggesting that these customary rules included restrictions on expressive activities.[6]

It may be true that our primitive ancestors did not conceptualize freedom as it is perceived now; nevertheless, they exercised freedom in its maximum extent. They may not have any conscious definition of freedom, nor may they hold any conception of it, but they were exercising all forms of it. This might have been the case for most of other concepts and notions.[7] Certainly, our primitive ancestors used gestures, symbolic expressions and all sorts of verbal communications freely, but they did not have a conception of free expression or communication. Thus, my intuition is that in the primitive human communities there was freedom without any conception of freedom, and there was absolute FoE without any reflection on justifying it.

Why was there no conception of freedom and no reflection on justifying free expression and communication in the state of nature? My simple answer is that there was no need for conceptualizing freedom, nor was there any need for reflection on justifying it because there was no direct, tangible power on and above freedom.[8] Humans lived freely in the absence of power and in the absence of social institutions and political organizations. Those who lived in isolation or with others, whether as a family or as any other natural or mutual bond, did not know any limitation of their expressive activities. Thus, they did not need to conceptualize the limit of their expressive activities and did not need to reflect on justifying the possible boundaries of their expressive activities. They draw on the wall of the caves whenever they wanted, however they could, and on

[6] For a brief account on ways of life and social structure among early humans, see section 9 of Bo Gräslund, *Early humans and their world* (Routledge, 2005)

[7] It is argued that the imagination of people in ancient times was completely covered by mythical views about themselves, nature, life, and their surroundings. This mythical state and the absence of any notion of progress and conceptualization arguably continued until the period of the emergence of philosophical inquiry in ancient Greek. See M. C. Lemon, *Philosophy of history: a guide for students* (Routledge, 2003)

[8] A more complicated answer to that question may consider the capacity of conceptualization by humans then. But I guess this reason is more technical than fundamental.

whatever things they imagined without knowing any limitation and without reflecting on the rightness or wrongness of the drawings.

It may not be proved that wherever and whenever there was no human society, religious institution, or political power, all imaginable expressive activities were permitted without any sort of justification within family members or other collective entities.[9] Nevertheless, it can be claimed that in rudimentary forms of human societies held together only by traditional rules of behaviour, there were no social institutions of power, no political organization, no restrictive rules for regulating expressive activities, and no existence of the interests restrictive to expressive activities. Accordingly, it is hard to imagine that expressive activities were limited, and that there was any conception of FoE or any reflection on justifying communicative activities in these primitive communities.

III. RELIGION AS THE FIRST AND OLDEST SOURCE OF RESTRICTING THE FREEDOM OF EXPRESSION

Primitive forms of mythologies, [10] superstitions, [11] and religions can be considered the oldest source of limitation on expressive activities.[12] I reached this arguable conclusion after reviewing and reflecting on a number of works written about the origins and

[9] State of nature

[10] In *'What is Mythology'* John Fisks elaborates the original meaning, description and definition of mythology. He writes 'The study of mythology, therefore, when properly conducted, must throw light on some of the early thoughts of mankind, giving us glimpses of the way in which people reasoned about things before there was any such knowledge of nature as we are accustomed to call scientific.' See John Fiske, 'What is Mythology?' (1881) 48 *Atlantic Monthly* 85

[11] Its original meaning was 'fear of demons.' See Ernst Riess, 'On Ancient Superstition' (1895) 26 *Transactions of the American Philological Association (1869-1896)* 40

[12] All religions without exception have had sacred rules and holy instructions about expressive activities, about what, how, when and where their followers must say or not to say. I doubt that there has been any religion without rules or instructions on humans' expressive choices. Some rules are positive requiring what must be expressed in forms of prayers or the like. Other rules might be negative requiring what must not be expressed.

history of superstition, mythology, and religion of primitive peoples.[13] In addition to survival thoughts, superstitious and religious thoughts appear to be among the few ideas that crossed the mind of the ancient people. I'm not a historian, but this should not disqualify me from making historical arguments based on intuitive reflections on recorded historical events and materials.

Superstitious ceremonials and religious rituals were common among primitive people and ancient families. They may have been practiced individually or collectively. They certainly involved different forms of expressive activities. The notion of power, natural or supernatural, appears to be behind those ceremonies and rituals. Whoever practiced a form of superstitious ceremony, religious ritual, or prayer may have done it to communicate with a form of power: real or mythical, visible or invisible, natural or supernatural. It may be difficult to identify the exact purpose of ancient men and families in performing a specific religious ritual or prayer; nevertheless, it is not difficult to locate some notion of communicating with a power in their mind whenever they performed the ritual.

When a father in the ancient times gathered the whole family to sit quietly around the fire during sunset and ended the ceremony with a collective recitation of a few verbal expressions, he lead the ceremony in the position of power and performed it to communicate with another more powerful being whatever it would have been in his imagination. Thus, when the notion of metaphysical power was born in the mind of people and when the forms of power were practiced among people, expressive activities started to become restricted. Then, people may have had to accept the power of father or grandfather, even when he is dead, as a source of life or as a god that can make laws

---

13 See Samuel Noah Kramer, *Mythologies of the ancient world* (Doubleday, 1961); H. C, 'ANCIENT ATHEISM AND SUPERSTITION' (1862) 1(1) *Journal of sacred literature and Biblical record, Apr.1855-Jan.1867* 24; Katharine Savage, *The history of world religions* (Bodley Head, 1966); David S. Noss, *A history of the world's religions* (Prentice Hall, 1999)

for life, and that must be obeyed and even worshiped by specific regular ceremonials.[14] This is how the religious rules of freedom may have started to control human life and freedom.

Who can convincingly prove that I make illusionary historical statements if I claim that five thousand years ago a son was killed by his father because he did not perform his regular expressive ritual around his grandfather's grave, a wife was abandoned because she made the god angry by expressing or not expressing something, or a brother was beaten because he spitted over his grandfather's grave out of anger. Thus, because there were the gods, sacred symbols of power, and rituals and prayers for the gods, it does not seem illogical to imagine that there were punishments for not conducting prayers or not performing the expressive activities required by the conventional duties to the gods or the symbols of their power.

In short, religion in its different forms may arguably be the first source of institutional power.[15] The seed of that power started to grow from primitive families, developed further with human settlements, became stronger after the emergence of communities and sects, and reached its peak when it became the foundation of social organizations and political institutions in society. Once different forms of religious institutions established, expressive activities, similar to all other forms of freedom, were restricted in a sense. For example, when a religious power within a family, a sect, a community or a settlement required performing a specific regular religious ritual or prayers, it can be imagined that no one was free not to do that. In that sense, people started to become less free once religion became an institutionalized power over freedom. Until then,

[14] For further details about the role of myths and religions in families, organising power within families, leading ceremonies and worships, and in introducing and enforcing various rules and laws in ancient times, see Numa Denis Fustel de Coulanges, *The ancient city: a study on the religion, laws, and institutions of Greece and Rome* (Doubleday, 1956)

[15] I tend to agree with the underlying argument of those who claim that 'religion, in early times, shapes the laws,' and that 'from religion came all laws and rules.' See ibid

humans were in the maximum possible state of freedom, and more importantly they did not have to justify their free activities to anyone, to any institution, or to any power. The justification of expressive activities presumably started to appear with the emergence of religious restrictions on expressive activities.

IV. THE EMERGENCE OF JUSTIFICATIONS AS REACTION TO RELIGIOUS RESTRICTIONS

The first restrictive laws of FoE were possibly religious in nature, and the first justificatory arguments for FoE were reactions to these restrictions. This may arguably be correct for most of the laws of freedom and other laws governing people's conducts. One strong argument among legal historians is that the source, nature and foundation of first laws were religious.[16] Michael Stolleis claims that what has been called 'the eye of the law or the eye of the justice' in 'almost all civilizations throughout time' initially has a metaphysical origin. Laws started with 'in the name of God.' Then, it has been gradually secularized.[17] A brief review of the historical records, relevant laws and practices existed in the ancient civilizations of Mesopotamia, Egypt, Athens and Rome illustrates that assumption.

In a study of religion and politics in ancient Egypt, Etim E. Okon concluded 'religion was indispensable in ancient Egypt. Religion and politics in ancient Egyptian society were inseparable. Ancient Egyptians were incurably religious. Social and political life was a religious phenomenon.'[18] In that collective life, no doubt that all written laws, if existed which is unlikely, customary laws and practices were also religious in nature.

16 It is important to avoid generalization about the religious nature of historical background and foundations of the laws of freedom because it may be problematic. Some laws of freedom such as laws against physical violence, theft and breaking promises probably pre-dated institutionalized religion.

17. See Michael Stolleis, *The eye of the law: two essays on legal history* (Birbeck Law, 2009)

18 See Etim Okon, 'Religion and politics in ancient Egypt' (2012) 3(3) *American Journal of Social and Management Sciences* 93

Accordingly, it can be concluded that restrictive laws, rules, or customs were mainly religious in nature. It is doubtful that people in ancient Egypt were free to challenge the highest political and sacred religious status of the Kings, Pharaoh. The story of Moses in the Quran narrates what happens to Moses after he challenged the religious status of Pharaoh and expressed his religious belief.[19]

Similarly, city-states in Mesopotamia were considered as 'the private property of the divine family.' They were governed by the temple lords who were 'both sacred-spiritual and secular leaders.'[20] Thus, it is convincingly argued 'temple was the center of power.'[21] It is unlikely that people were free to express what would have been considered unreligious.[22]

Regarding ancient Athens, it is well recorded that there were legal restrictions on expressive conducts on various accounts.[23] There were various versions of libel law. As Max Radin indicates, some expressions were considered 'unsayable.' From his review of the ancient Athenian laws, he finds that according to the laws existed then 'one might not say that a man had thrown away his shield in battle, that he had slain anyone, or that he had beaten his father or his mother.'[24] Despite the existence of some laws regulating

---

[19] See P Gheiasvand and Nia AB Taheri, 'Repettition of the Story of Moses & Pharaoh in the Holy Quran ' (2010) *LITERARY CULTURE QUARTERLY*

[20] See Robert Chadwick, *First civilizations: ancient Mesopotamia and ancient Egypt* (Equinox Pub, 2005)

[21] Ibid

[22] This is only my intuitive perspective. The article 127 of the Hammurabi Code says 'If a man point the finger at a priestess or the wife of another and cannot justify it, they shall drag that man before the judges and they shall brand his forehead.' King of Babylonia Hammurabi and Robert Francis Harper, *The code of Hammurabi, King of Babylon, about 2250 B.C: autographed text, transliteration, translation, glossary, index of subjects, lists of proper names, signs, numerals, corrections, and erasures with map, frontispiece and photograph of text* (University of Chicago Press ; New York, 1904)Even though it does not directly support my perspective, it does not also refute it. It was mainly a code to regulate the conducts between individuals in their daily life. Most of the laws and rules that we call constitution and regulate relationship between power and freedom were unwritten in ancient time. This is where the religious rules of FoE can be found.

[23] For a detailed study on the practice of FoE and the root of its limits in ancient Athens, see Arlene W. Saxonhouse, *Free speech and democracy in ancient Athens* (Cambridge University Press, 2006)

[24] See Max Radin, 'Freedom of Speech in Ancient Athens' (1927) 48(3) *The American Journal of Philology* 215

expressive conducts between individuals, the real and serious restriction on FoE was the restriction existed to regulate expressive activities of individuals in relation to the religious authority whether it was mystical or political. If the penalty of expressing unsayable expressions or libellous expressions against other individuals was a fine of five hundred drachmae, the punishment of expressing impiety was death. Thus, the most serious restriction on FoE in ancient Athens was religious in nature.[25] To understand that more clearly, one needs no more than reading Plato's Apology of Socrates and Euthyphro dialogue.[26]

In the Apology, Plato eloquently narrates the trial of Socrates in 399 BC. By reflecting on the Apology, one can easily sense a strong presence of religion and the gods in the Athenian law, culture, thinking, as well as in the Athenian restriction on expressive activities based on religion considerations. This is behind the charge brought against Socrates. 'Socrates is guilty of corrupting the young and of not believing in the gods in whom the city believes, but in other new spiritual things.'[27] From the dialogues, one can conclude that while the major restriction on FoE during that time was a religious restriction, the major justification of FoE was based on seeking for knowledge and searching for the truth. Socrates' trial and execution illustrate that.

In his trial, he stands firmly against existing restrictive religious rules on freedom of seeking knowledge, searching for truth, engaging in philosophical arguments, and communicating with others for learning, educating, and spreading the virtues. He firmly tells the Athenians that 'If I say that it is impossible for me to keep quiet because that

25 There are other non-religious analyses for understanding exercise of FoE and its limits. Athenian democracy, as a political consideration, and Athenian philosophical dialogues- as an intellectual considerations- have also been considered as the base for understanding the nature of FoE in ancient Greek. See Enrico Berti, 'Ancient Greek Dialectic as Expression of Freedom of Thought and Speech' (1978) 39(3) *Journal of the History of Ideas* 347
26 Plato (Edit: John M. Cooper & D.S. Hutchinson), *Plato complete works* (Hackett, 1997)
27 Ibid

means disobeying the god, you will not believe me and will think I'm being ironical. On the other hand, if I say that it is the greatest good for a man to discuss virtue every day and those other things about which you hear me conversing and testing myself and others, for the unexamined life is not worth living for men, you will believe me even less.'[28]

Despite executing Socrates mainly because of exercising FoE, one may still argue that it is not reasonable to charge the entire Athenian democracy at that time for being against FoE. It may be argued that ancient Athenian democracy was among the best political systems in the world for respecting FoE of all its citizens, and that humanity has inherited the concept of FoE from that golden age of Athenian democracy.[29] It was a form of direct democracy based on the political expression. The Athenians were conducting whatever artistic, athletic, cultural, religious and cultural expressive activities they desired in the Agora.[30] Accordingly, it can be concluded that FoE was the principal pillar of Athenian democracy.[31] If that was how they made the Agora a central place for expressive activities, how can we describe the ancient Greek city-state of Athens as an example for introducing religious restrictions on FoE to the humanity?[32]

In response, I must start by reiterating the structure of my whole argument about the historical background of the justifications of FoE. My assumption is that initially humans were in a maximum condition of FoE. Before the emergence of religious or superstitious

[28] Ibid

[29] Richard Allsop, for example, claims that the concept of FoE can be traced back to the ancient Greeks. 'One of the first steps on the Greek path towards allowing FoE was the first involvement of ordinary people in intellectual life.' Richard Allsop, 'The difficult history of free speech' (2012) 56(Generic) *Quadrant Magazine* 55

[30] S. C. Todd, *Athens and Sparta* (Bristol Classical Press, 1996)

[31] See Saxonhouse, above n ; Radin, above n

[32] One possible answer can be found in what a writer observes which is ' FoE was linked to democratic deliberation, not individual rights in Athens.' Saxonhouse, above n Accordingly, in Ancient Athens FoE was part of- and based on- collective interests and public interests. Similarly, it was limited and restricted based on the foundation of democratic interests that protect the city as a collective entity. Certainly respecting the Gods was among the highest interests because the Gods were considered as the source of power and the protector of the city.

beliefs within primitive families, freedom of expressive activities may have been limitless; there was no limit, nor was there any need for justification for that matter. After the emergence of religious beliefs among primitive families and after the emergence of human settlements, communities, sects, and later social organizations and political institutions in the ancient times, FoE started to lose its limitless status because of the restrictive religious rules that gradually took place and found strength among the families and within the communities.

Therefore, religion can be considered as the first source of imposing restriction on expressive activities because it was the base of power in the families, and it was the foundation of authority in the various communities existed at that time. This can be observed in the ancient Greek city-states, especially Athens. Despite the remarkable democratic deliberation practiced in the Agora, there were a few legally restrictive rules on expressive activities; not offending the Olympian Gods, such as Zeus and Apollo, was among the strictest rules on FoE. Offending or 'questioning the divine was not part of Parrhe'sia.'[33] It is an Athenian phrase or word which means FoE or 'frank speech.'[34] Impious expressive activities were considered as offences against the gods and the city, and as such, those who were charged with impiety, such as Socrates, would face the harshest punishment and execution.

The offence of impiety was both religious and political in nature because at that time mythology, superstition and religion were integral and inseparable parts of the cultural life, political structure, and legal system of Athens. Likewise, the justification developed to defend FoE against the charge of impiety and against the religious-political authority of Athens was both religious and political in nature. By reading the Apology and Crito, one can easily conclude that the first well-developed argument for the justification of

33 Ibid
34 Ibid

FoE was formulated by Socrates. The justificatory argument or theory was a defence of FoE against religious restrictions; it was founded on seeking knowledge and searching for truth, and it was substantively grounded on the idea of justice.[35]

Similarly, in the Roman Empire there were religious restrictions on FoE. The restrictions were both religious and political in nature. Blasphemy is a clear example. It was one of the most common, widely practiced, and harshly punishable restrictions on FoE. Based on blasphemy, a big portion of humans' FoE has been outlawed for centuries. Because it 'included the use or abuse of language, or behavioral acts, that scorn the existence, nature, or power of sacred being,'[36] it excluded almost all non-conventional expressions or publications which were not directly approved by religious institutions of power from FoE. It criminalized expressing or publishing anything which were considered disrespectful to the God, his messages, his laws of life, his symbols, his sacred representatives and his earthly institutions of power, such as temples, churches, assembly houses, etc.[37] The nature of what were considered blasphemous crimes indicates that those crimes designed to restrict FoE based on religious considerations.

V. THE CO-EVOLVEMENT OF INSTITUTIONAL POWER AND THE JUSTIFICATIONS OF THE FREEDOM OF EXPRESSION

Justifications of FoE have evolved in parallel with the manifestation of power in both religious and political institutions. The justifications were born immediately after political powers emerged; their nature changed with the changes occurred in the nature of political power. When the Greek philosopher and one of the founders of Cynicism

---

35 See Plato, *Plato: Complete Works* (Hackett Publishing Co, Inc, 1997)

36 David Nash, 'Analyzing the History of Religious Crime. Models of "Passive" and "Active" Blasphemy since the Medieval Period' (2007) 41(1) *Journal of Social History [H.W.Wilson - SSA]* 5

37 For a detailed analysis of the history of blasphemy, see Leonard W. Levy, *Treason against God: a history of the offense of blasphemy* (Schocken Books, 1981)

Diogenes of Sinope told Alexander the Great to 'stop blocking his sunlight,' [38] he implied what political power has done to freedom. Before the emergence of political powers, freedom of expressive activities appeared to have been significantly, if not absolutely, unfettered and uncontrolled. With the gradual emergence of political powers, with the establishment of political systems, kings, leaders, law-making institutions, and empires, the circle of individual freedoms has been gradually shrunk.[39] Freedom started to suffer once different forms of political powers emerged and started to control and subordinate humans' free will.

The historical origin of political power is a complex and controversial issue. What, when, and where was the first appearance or manifestation of power, how it came to exist, why humans submitted themselves to the will of others and agreed to chain their freedom to others, how did the first ever kings, princes, lords, and leaders came to exist, and based on what they justified their coercive power are among the controversial questions about the historical origin of power. What is not controversial, however, is the adverse effect of political institutions of power, in all its forms, on human freedom. The effects have been very harsh. Humanity was introduced to power after being born free; nonetheless, humans were, and still are, compelled to bow the knee and plea for their natural entitlement of freedom in front of different institutions and symbols of power. Socrates had to plead for his freedom to speak in front of the Athenian institution of mixed religious-political power, Diogenes had to cynically remind Alexander the Great to stop blocking the sunlight of life and freedom, and both Christians and afterwards non-

[38] John Christian Laursen, 'Cynicism as an Ideology Behind Freedom of Expression in Denmark-Norway' in Elizabeth Powers (ed), *Freedom of Speech: The History of an Idea* (Bucknell University Press, 2011)
[39] For some aspects of FoE after the emergence and establishment of political institutions in classical antiquity, see Ineke Sluiter and Ralph Mark Rosen, *Free speech in classical antiquity:[Penn-Leiden Colloquium on Ancient Values, June 2002 at the University of Pennsylvania]* (Brill, 2004)

believers had to justify and fight for their expressive activities in front of the ancient Roman laws and the judges.[40]

Many centuries later, a combination of religious and political power was the reason behind the 'first consistent articulation' of the arguments of FoE in England, Holland, France and other parts of Europe.[41] It may not be inaccurate to claim that both Renaissance and Enlightenment were comprehensive intellectual movements against the religious-political institutions of power for the sake of protecting all forms of human freedom including FoE. The major roots of the modern theories and justifications of FoE can be found in the arguments put forward by the intellectual leaders of both Renaissance and Enlightenment.[42] Their arguments were mainly based on the value of freedom, limit of the power and religious tolerance.[43]John Milton wrote *Areopagitica* to defend FoE against the forms of censorship and licensing practiced by the institutions of power.[44] Similarly, John Stuart Mill defended FoE by claiming for the marketplace of ideas so that everyone can exchange ideas freely about all imaginable topics of life, including truth, god and power.[45]

---

[40] For some examples see F. H. Cramer, 'Bookburning and Censorship in Ancient Rome' (1945) 6(1) *Journal of the History of Ideas* 157

[41] Elizabeth Powers claims 'it was in England and Holland that the arguments for FoE received their first consistent articulation.' See Elizabeth Powers, *Freedom of speech: the history of an idea* (Bucknell University Press, 2011)

[42] FoE practices were also common political and social practices in sixteenth-century Spanish America. See Lewis Hanke, 'Free Speech in Sixteenth-Century Spanish America' (1946) 26(2) *The Hispanic American Historical Review* 135

[43] In the 16th century, which is arguably marked as the first historical stage of developing FoE theories, FoE was initially considered and treated as an aspect of religious tolerance. See Joris Van Eijnatten, 'In Praise of Moderate Enlightenment: A taxonomy of Early Modern Arguments in favour of Freedom of Expression ' in Elizabeth Powers (ed), *Freedom of speech: the history of an idea* (Bucknell University Press, 2011) This may prove that FoE was initially defended by begging religious powers and institutions for being tolerant with those express their different opinions regarding religion and other issues.

[44] See John Milton and John Wesley Hales, *Areopagitica* (Clarendon Press, 1886) For a guide to better understand Milton's *Areopagitica*, see Willmoore Kendall, 'How to Read Milton's Areopagitica' (1960) 22(1) *Journal of Politics* 439

[45] See chapter II of John Stuart Mill, *On liberty* (Prometheus Books, 1986) For some arguments on Mill's account of FoE, see K. C. O'Rourke, *John Stuart Mill and freedom of expression: the genesis of a theory* (Routledge, 2001); T. D. Campbell, 'John Stuart Mill and Freedom of Speech' (1971) 4(3) *Pensiero politico* 443; John

In making pleas for freedom and providing justifications for FoE, those philosophers never assumed that human freedom needs justification. Their arguments were about the limits of power, not about the moral justification of FoE.[46] Both Renaissance and Enlightenment can be considered as the cultural and intellectual movements of direct criticism against power, more than movements for providing justification for life and freedom. FoEs in general and freedom of the press, communication or publication, in particular, was among the most significant issues defended by intellectuals during Enlightenment mainly because they wanted to stand firmly against institutions of power.[47] Based on that same rationale, some writers argue 'Enlightenment was an age of criticism; it meant the fearless application of reason to society's institutions, practices, and beliefs.'[48]

Generally, what compelled great thinkers in history to provide justifications for freedom was not that they doubted the moral foundation of freedom or that they did not believe in freedom as an end in itself. Rather, they attempted to defend freedom based on the same artificial rationales used by institutions of power to restrict freedom.[49] This is what Socrates, Milton, Mill and others have tried to accomplish by developing justificatory theories of FoE.

Michael Roberts, 'John Stuart Mill, free speech and the public sphere: a Bakhtinian critique' (2004) 52 *The Sociological review* 67; R. George Wright, 'A Rationale from J. S. Mill for the Free Speech Clause' (1985) 1985 *The Supreme Court Review* 149; Paul A. Passavant, 'A Moral Geography of Liberty: John Stuart Mill and American Free Speech Discourse' (1996) 5(4) *Social & Legal Studies* 301; Alan Haworth, 'On Mill, Infallibility, and Freedom of Expression' (2007) 13(1) *Res Publica* 77

46 See Mill, above n ; Milton and Hales, above n

47 See Leonard W. Levy, *Emergence of a free press* (Oxford University Press, 1985) (This book partly presents the struggle of FoE and press with institutions of power. It indirectly tells the story behind the development of justifications and laws of FoE and the press).

48 See Lemon, above n

49 For a brief historical background of the development of FoE arguments, see Allsop, above n

For example, Mill wrote *On Liberty* to stand firmly against religious intolerance which was an integrated part of the political and social tyranny existed during his time.[50] In a thorough examination of Mill's account of FoE, it has been concluded that Mill had two major tasks. First, in articulating his theory of free expression, Mill's aim was to eradicate the various forms of religious intolerance practiced during his time. Second, Mill wanted to lay a strong foundation for freedom as the most effective means of attaining well-being and achieving maximum happiness.[51]

VI. CONCLUSION

After centuries of theoretical clash between power and freedom, it has now become necessary to reflect on the nature and source of this historical clash so that we can easily locate the theoretical problems we have inherited. After such reflection, one would not have difficulty to argue that different institutions of power must be fettered by considerations of human life and freedom, that no god has vested any divine authority in anyone or any institution to control humans' life and freedom, that freedom is the source of legitimacy of authorities, that the legitimacy of authority needs to be convincingly justified, that freedom- in all forms- requires no moral justification, but rather, power and authorities- in all forms- must be convincingly justified.

My final comment here is that despite the current trend of justificatory theories of free speech, and despite the attractiveness of some of the theories of justifications, we must be cautious in adopting those theories and in embracing their features. We must not continue taking the justificatory roads engineered by the defending pioneers of freedom. They designed justifications for free speech based on seeking knowledge, searching for

50 For some explanatory, analytical, and guiding works about *On Liberty*, see C. L. Ten, *Mill's On liberty: a critical guide* (Cambridge University Press, 2008); Gerald Dworkin, *Mill's On liberty: critical essays* (Rowman & Littlefield Publishers, 1997); Peter Radcliff, *Limits of liberty: studies of Mill's On liberty* (Wadsworth, 1966)

51 Uner Daglier, *John Stuart Mill's two-pronged argument for freedom of expression* (Dissertation/Thesis Thesis, ProQuest, UMI Dissertations Publishing, 2005)

truth, finding truth and defeating falsehood in the marketplace of ideas because these arguments were by many standards one of the only two available effective options they have in order to fight for freedom against almighty political powers.

When an almighty power dominates all aspects of life and controls all forms of freedom, there are only two ways to fight for life and freedom. The first one is an offensive way, and the second is defensive. While the former way refers to attacking the nature, foundation and forms of the power through questioning its legitimacy, and criticizing its foundation, the latter way is to defend life and freedom through providing moral justifications of life and freedom. Historically, the justifications of freedom of expressions were developed as part of the defensive approach taken by the thinkers to defend freedom.[52] Despite the long history of that approach, and despite its relative effects on defending freedom against power throughout history, we must no longer consider that approach.

If we want to take freedom of expression seriously, a theoretical defensive approach is not the most effective option. Old justificatory theories of freedom of expression and even the recent theories, built on the elements of the old ones, have all missed a very crucial point about freedom. Power over freedom requires justification, not vice versa. To take freedom of expression seriously, the focal question regarding freedom of expression should be different from the historical justificatory questions. My understanding is that if we continue asking 'why does freedom of speech deserve legal protection?' nothing significant can be achieved practically and theoretically. Instead, a more fundamental question must dominate jurisprudential discussions about free speech which is 'why is freedom of speech restricted?'

[52] In the 16th century, which is arguably marked as the first historical stage of developing free speech theories, freedom of speech was initially considered and treated as an aspect of religious tolerance. See Eijnatten, above n This may prove that free speech was initially defended through begging religious powers and institution for being tolerance with those who speak their mind and express their opinions.

Some may argue that this latter question is an important question for freedom in general, but the other question, namely why does freedom of speech deserve legal protection?, is a more significant question of freedom of speech because with reflecting on that question the special value of free speech, not freedom in general, can be examined. In other words, some may argue that justifications of freedom of speech have been historically initiated and recently reiterated and developed further not based on the belief that there is a need for moral justification of freedom in general, but based on the assumption that there is a special value in free speech which requires special moral theorization and special legal protection. Is that so? The answer is positive for those who argue that there is freedom of speech principle to some extent independent from the general principle of freedom. However, I doubt the existence of such problematic and baseless principle.

Of Mosquitoes and Men: The Basis of Animal and Human Rights

Jasper Doomen

Abstract

This article discusses the status of animal rights, and more particularly whether these rights may be defended from a natural rights perspective or from an ethical perspective. I argue that both options fail. The same analysis applies in the case of mankind. 'Mankind' does not bring with it the acknowledgement such rights, nor does a focus on what is arguably characteristic of mankind, namely, reason. Reason is decisive, though, in another respect, namely, the fact that reasonable beings can claim and lay down rights. It does not follow from this that animals should have no rights, since human beings may be motivated to constitute such rights, while this provides the most solid basis for them.

Introduction

In the wake of an ever stronger relativization of the differences between human beings and (other) animals, it has become increasingly difficult to separate a domain of rights to which only human beings should be entitled. It seems difficult to deny that human rights should be acknowledged without also granting the relevant rights to animals, 'relevant' indicating that some rights, such as the right to vote, are of no use to them. Indeed, if one seeks to take a moral stance, this distinction has come under pressure. It is possible to focus on what presumably uniquely characterizes mankind, namely, reason, but it remains to be seen whether this position is tenable.

In section 1, I present an important argument for those who plead acknowledging rights for animals, or, similarly, treating animals well on the basis of moral considerations, namely, the argument from marginal cases, after which I indicate why focusing on mankind as such, i.e., without it being clear which criterion or criteria would purportedly warrant a special treatment, is a cul-de-sac.

Section 2 presents reason as a potential candidate. Kant's view of practical reason as a special faculty is contrasted with an account of reason that does not treat it as something the existence of which *eo ipso* warrants a certain treatment for those endowed with it, but starts from the more realistic and better supportable perspective that reason is simply a faculty that cannot be ignored when granting rights is concerned. The interests of human beings must be taken to heart (by those same human beings) since not doing so would either be inconsistent or unfeasible, or both.

The third section discusses the consequences of this outlook, taking into consideration alternatives such as Singer's. A position that starts from moral dictates is not outright dismissed, but such dictates cannot be decisive as long as it is unclear how they might motivate actions.

1. Animals vis-à-vis human beings

The issue of whether animals are entitled to a certain treatment on the basis of the acknowledgment of animal rights or moral considerations is an important one, which has been answered in the affirmative by many, from diverse considerations. There are differences of opinion whether animal *rights* or rather animal *interests* should be the focus of attention, but this is in fact a minor issue as long as their arguments to promote these rights or interests stem from the same motivation for the reason that those who plead animal interests would, presumably, want to transpose those interests into rights. The crucial issue would then be whether things like (natural) rights may be said to exist irrespective of their being realized through a process of legislation. While those who focus on animal interests are not plagued by the justification problem of proving that such rights exist, at least if their claim is that animal interests consist in something that can be demonstrated relatively easily, such as their suffering being ended or prevented, they, too, face the burden of proving on what foundation a moral appeal to those who might remove such suffering should be based. I will return to this issue below.

In any event, if one starts from a moral appeal, the argument from marginal cases,[1] meaning that the dividing line between animals on the one hand and cognitively impaired people (and maybe children) on the other cannot consistently be maintained, those clinging to it being accused of 'speciesism', seems difficult to dispel: "[...] those who think moral status does depend on capacity X are forced to draw one of two conclusions. Either they will have to admit that marginal humans do not have moral status because they do not have capacity X. Or if they wish to maintain that marginal humans have moral status they must admit that it depends on something other than capacity X. If this something else is a feature which animals share it must be admitted that animals have moral status too."[2]

There appear to be three options. It may be argued, first, that humans have natural rights (or moral status) while animals do not; second, that both humans *and* animals have such rights; and third, that *none* have such rights. Those who take the argument from marginal cases seriously would not prefer the second option to the first, but it does not follow from that given that the third option

[1] J. Narveson, "Animal Rights", p. 164.
[2] J. Tanner, "The Marginal Cases Argument: Animals Matter Too", pp. 53, 54.

should not be preferred to both. Indeed, there are reasons to consider it the superior alternative, which are persuasive enough to do so, as I will argue.

A strategy to remedy this problem may be to shift the focus from the individual to the species to which it belongs, which includes even individuals who have lost the presumably relevant characteristic or have never had it to begin with. Kateb maintains such a position, by distinguishing between the status of individuals and the stature of the human race.[3] Human dignity is defended by Kateb by pointing to both aspects.[4] No human beings are thus excluded, providing Kateb with the opportunity to state: "There are people who are so disabled that they cannot function. Does the idea of dignity apply to them? Yes, they remain human beings in the most important respect. If they cannot actively exercise many or any of their rights they nevertheless retain a right to life, whatever their incapacities (short of the most extreme failures of functioning)."[5]

The difficulties become apparent from the following: "I am not saying that when we regard any particular individual we should see in him or her an embodiment or personification of the whole human record, and by that conceit inflate the person into the species, or even allow the full range of demonstrated human capacity to bestow its aura on any given human being or on all human beings equally. No, we deal here with the stature of the species, carrying with it a past that grew out of other species and will be extended indefinitely into the future. But the fact remains that every individual has all the uniquely human traits and attributes that the human record shows. The human record shows and will show, however, a cumulative display of these traits and attributes that surpasses any

[3] G. Kateb, *Human Dignity*, p. 6.
[4] G. Kateb, *Human Dignity*, p. 9.
[5] G. Kateb, *Human Dignity*, p. 19.

individual and any particular group or society."[6] The issue resulting from the argument from marginal cases is not, then, resolved by Kateb.[7]

Even if the argument from marginal cases is disregarded (if only *arguendo*), those who argue that special moral duties should apply in the case of human beings compared to animals may not, or at least not yet, consider their distinction justified, for they are still faced with the burden to prove, first, *what* makes human beings special, i.e., what quality or qualities single them out, and, second, *why* such a quality or qualities should be sufficient reason to be treated in a special way. In the next section, I will discuss a candidate that has often been proffered: reason.

2. The import of reason

Reason seems to be the only quality that can consistently be presented as the relevantly distinguishing one between animals and human beings. Kant is perhaps the most important promoter of such a position. It must be said that Kant does not consider understanding, or reasoning power, the decisive feature: for him, 'reason' in the sense of *practical* reason is what distinguishes man in the decisive respect from animal; understanding does lead to a difference, but this is a relative difference,[8] which is primarily important in private law. The role of practical reason becomes clear from Kant's remark that one is to be considered an end in itself on the basis of being autonomous,[9] which is (supposedly)

[6] G. Kateb, *Human Dignity*, pp. 125, 126.

[7] Besson's position is equally void: "[…] *human* rights are universal moral rights of a special intensity that belong to all human beings by virtue of their humanity. Human rights are universal moral rights because the interests they protect belong to all human beings." S. Besson, "International Human Rights and Political Equality: Some Implications for Global Democracy", p. 97.

[8] I. Kant, *Grundlegung zur Metaphysik der Sitten*, pp. 434-436; *Die Metaphysik der Sitten*, pp. 435, 436.

[9] I. Kant, *Kritik der praktischen Vernunft*, p. 87. Elsewhere (*Grundlegung zur Metaphysik der Sitten*, p. 440), Kant defines autonomy (of the will) as "the quality of the will by which it is a law to itself (independently of any quality of the objects of volition)." ("[…] die Beschaffenheit des Willens,

possible in the domain that one cannot reach on the basis of – theoretical – reason.[10] (Since this limitation is in place, I say 'supposedly'.) So the understanding (or reasoning power) does not constitute the decisive ground for man to be considered an end in itself; a being rather has 'dignity' on the basis of its capacity to act morally.[11] Autonomy is the basis of the 'dignity' of man, and of every reasonable creature (or 'nature', in Kant's words).[12]

Rather than elaborate on the problems involved with Kant's defense of practical reason in particular, I will focus on what is decisive for the present discussion, which is the issue of the connection between being endowed with reason (or another quality) and being treated in a special way.

Such a connection is not evident. For example, it may be argued that those who are endowed with reason and who are in addition especially intelligent may use their abilities to display skills where others are unable to do so, resulting in, for example, different incomes, but that situation must not be confused with the present one, which is concerned with the question of whether different treatment should follow from the quality *eo ipso*, and on what *such a connection* would be based, if anything, is unclear.

McGinn rightly adduces the contingent factors that have led to human domination over animals while not being dominated by other beings,[13] but while this may necessitate a reassessment of mankind's special position vis-à-vis animals, or at least some of them, it is not clear why a moral obligation towards

---

dadurch derselbe ihm selbst (unabhängig von aller Beschaffenheit der Gegenstände des Wollens) ein Gesetz ist.")

[10] E.g. I. Kant, *Kritik der reinen Vernunft*, A 532 ff./B 560 ff., A 702/B 730, A 800 ff./B 828 ff.

[11] I. Kant, *Grundlegung zur Metaphysik der Sitten*, p. 435.

[12] "*Autonomy* is the basis of the dignity of human and every reasonable nature." ("*Autonomie* ist [...] der Grund der Würde der menschlichen und jeder vernünftigen Natur.") I. Kant, *Grundlegung zur Metaphysik der Sitten*, p. 436.

[13] C. McGinn, "Apes, Humans, Aliens, Vampires and Robots", pp. 147-149.

such beings would follow from that consideration. Self-interest may provide a more compelling foundation here: one imagines oneself oppressed and would want to avoid certain experiences that accompany such a situation. In practical terms, this may alter some of mankind's relations with (some) animals, as will be indicated in section 3, but that does not touch upon the present issue of the supposedly moral foundation.

Jamieson's position is similarly problematic. He says: "[…] the community of equals is the moral community within which certain basic moral principles govern our relations with each other; and these moral principles include the right to life and the protection of individual liberty."[14] A community of equals may be defended: different beings should be treated equally, at least in some respects, on account of the fact that their differences should be considered irrelevant. The step from that given to a supposedly 'moral community', however, is in need of justification. By contrast, if the appeal to equal treatment may be based on self-interest, no such elements need to be added.

The same consideration applies to what Regan[15] and Francione[16] observe. As is clear from these quotes, the present considerations apply irrespective of whether one starts from a rights-based approach or from an interests-based one. In both cases, a moral criterion is put forward as decisive, without indicating what this

---

[14] D. Jamieson, "Great Apes and the Human Resistance to Equality", p. 224.

[15] T. Regan, "Narveson on Egoism and the Rights of Animals", p. 186: "It is […] the capacity to suffer itself that seems to provide the only adequate grounds for attributing the right in question to those humans, including morons, to whom we wish to attribute it. It is because, like us, morons can suffer, that they, like us, seem to have as much claim as we do to the right not to be made to do so gratuitously."

[16] G. Francione, "Animals – Property or Persons?", p. 121: "[…] if we are to make good on our claim to take animal interests seriously, then we can do so only one way: by applying the *principle of equal consideration* – the rule that we ought to treat like cases alike unless there is a good reason not to do so – to animals. The principle of equal consideration is a necessary component of every moral theory. […] Although there may be many differences between humans and animals, there is at least one important similarity that we all already recognize: our shared capacity to suffer."

means, let alone on what this would supposedly be based. The first part – i.e., what this means – *may* be said to be clear: isn't it morally right to keep other beings, among which animals, from suffering? To this I would respond that one may at best appeal to something as vague as an 'intuition'; perhaps more troubling, moral appeals may simply be dismissed, as no means to *enforce* such appeals are available lest those appeals not be moral, of course: it is in the nature of such appeals that one should not act upon them from exterior considerations.[17] What an alternative, 'interior' appeal, perhaps doing the right thing 'for its own sake', may mean I do not profess to know, and remains, I would add, a source of confusion and obscurity. The alternative to argue from self-interest appears to provide a more solid ground to reach the same effects.

This alternative leaves room to distinguish between human beings and animals in some important respects. Reason is, in this approach, the decisive factor, although reason is not a decisive *moral* characteristic, as it is with Kant. It is rather the feature that makes it possible to realize an outcome efficiently, the outcome in the present case being the alleviation of one's own suffering, and that of other beings, if one has an interest to do so. Crucially, reason is not only the faculty on the basis of which one recognizes that suffering must be alleviated (and the fact that such suffering may in fact remain to a great extent takes away nothing from that observation), but it is arguably simultaneously the decisive characteristic to be granted certain rights, on account of two, possibly related considerations.

[17] As Kant says: "Insofar the laws of freedom only refer to purely external actions and their conformity to the law, they are called *juridical*; do they also demand that they should themselves be the determining principles of the actions, they are *ethical*; and then one says: the conformity to the former is the *legality* of the action, while the conformity to the latter is its *morality*." ("So fern [die Gesetze der Freiheit] nur auf bloße äußere Handlungen und deren Gesetzmäßigkeit gehen, heißen sie *juridisch*; fordern sie aber auch, daß sie (die Gesetze) selbst die Bestimmungsgründe der Handlungen sein sollen, so sind sie *ethisch*, und alsdann sagt man: die Übereinstimmung mit den ersteren ist die *Legalität*, die mit den zweiten die *Moralität* der Handlung.") I. Kant, *Die Metaphysik der Sitten*, p. 214; cf. pp. 219, 225.

First, those who have reason would, if they were oppressed by others (who themselves act on the basis of reason, oppressing those others out of an interest, such as an economic interest[18]), have an interest to rise up against their oppressors, which may result in upheaval or even a civil war. This is sufficient reason for those in power not to oppress others. Slavery was admittedly not abolished in the U.S.A. because slaves themselves protested against their treatment, but black people still being treated unequally with white people thereafter, to which they responded with nonviolent *and* violent protests, did contribute to the Civil Rights Act of 1964. The policies of segregation that had been installed had been shown to have become corrupted, since it had become clear that black people were powerful and endowed with reason, both characteristics being intertwined in the sense that pure physical power would not have been sufficient, as some animals are far more powerful than any human being, while this is apparently no reason to grant them any rights. Before black people had the resolute to stand up for themselves or were simply not in a position to be able to do so, they were not treated equally. It might have been possible to leave the policies resisting equal treatment in place, as similar policies would remain in place in South Africa, but that might have resulted, in the worst case, in civil war.[19]

Second, for those who have reason to claim certain rights on that basis – in this case from the consideration that reason would *eo ipso* be the relevant moral characteristic to be granted such rights while excluding other beings lacking such

[18] This is no academic issue, as slavery is an important historical institution, having been abolished in the U.S.A. as recently as 1865, while black people were oppressed until far into the 20th century.

[19] I do not discuss here the criticism from other countries (such criticism being directed, incidentally, at South Africa in the 20th century, of course). After all, the fact that they would protest the policies would merely shift the question and would not provide an answer to the fundamental question that would still remain, namely, why those countries that oppose the policies would do so, and not implement them themselves, instead of acknowledging equal treatment as they have done.

a characteristic – would mean their contradicting themselves. This is sufficient to counter Singer's remark that reason (or rationality) would be an arbitrary characteristic.[20] It may be considered thus in moral terms, but I have already addressed that option, not starting from any supposedly moral characteristic.

I mentioned that these considerations are possibly related. By this I mean to say that they may together constitute the most plausible explanation in indicating why reason is the crucial factor. It does not by itself command respect for those who are able to act on it, unless respect is taken to mean simply that those who are endowed with reason cannot be overpowered, at least not easily. 'Power' has a broad meaning here, for those who are physically handicapped or weak are relevant beings, just as those who are potentially rational[21] (most children) or fictitiously so (the mentally handicapped, including extreme cases such as anencephalic children). In the latter case, of course, the power is vicarious in the sense that the power of those that protect them is what is decisive; the protection need not be provided by individuals (such as the parents of mentally handicapped or even 'normal' children), since on the basis of the foregoing analysis anyone may be said to have an interest in protecting them, so that it would be provided collectively.

This argument may be leveled against those who present the argument from marginal cases. It must be granted that the fictitious cases can be extended to include animals; whether the same consideration may in future times apply to the case of potentially rational beings I cannot say – if certain animals should at some point become (potentially) rational, what is argued here applies to them *for that reason*. Incidentally, reason is not to be equated with intelligence, since a certain

---

[20] P. Singer, *Practical Ethics*, p. 50.

[21] 'Reason' and 'rationality' are identified here. They may mean many things, but I will not needlessly complicate matters.

degree of intelligence is sufficient to constitute reason and thus being eligible to the right under discussion – the right to be treated equally, which not only prohibits discrimination but protects citizens, or, more generally, legal subjects, against being killed, while various degrees of intelligence may lead to being treated justifiably differently in some cases; for instance, those who have an above average intelligence can, *ceteris paribus*, earn more money than those that have an average or below-average intelligence.

Applying the fiction not only to mentally handicapped people but to animals, too, is certainly possible (if only because a fiction does not refer to a real state of affairs but is, *ex natura rei*, a product of one's own making), but apart from cases such as one's affection to a pet it would be difficult to see what would be a consideration here, while in the case of mentally handicapped people, such a consideration is evident: "While species, as such, has nothing to do with the case at the level of foundations, there are reasons of a straightforward kind for extending the ambit of morality to infants and morons, etc. We want to extend it to children because most of us want to have our own children protected, etc., and have really nothing to gain from being permitted to invade the children of others; we have an interest in the children of others being properly cared for, because we don't want them growing up to be criminals or delinquents, etc. (and we do want them to be interesting and useful people). And we shall want the feeble-minded generally respected because we ourselves might become so, as well as out of respect for their rational relatives who have a sentimental interest in these cases."[22] Only those who believe in reincarnation may be motivated to apply the fiction more broadly than this. A similar stance is presented by Posner: "It is because *we* are humans that we put humans first. If we were cats, we would

[22] J. Narveson, "Animal Rights", p. 177.

put cats first, regardless of what philosophers might tell us. Reason doesn't enter."[23]

Since reason is both the characteristic of those who may decide to treat beings in a certain way and the characteristic they consider crucial (on the basis of self-interest, if I am correct), reason is significant in two respects. First, it is what the beings who are able to assert rights share in common (which is an actual given, so that this may be called 'factual equality', and more specifically 'basic equality', in order to specify the decisive characteristic, which is reason, so that basic equality may in turn be specified by 'basic rationality'), and, second, it is the characteristic that is decisive in determining the extent of equal treatment (which may be called 'prescriptive equality'). So the same beings that are able to decide which beings should be treated equally are those to whom equal treatment is applied. Singer seems to overlook the fact that these two levels must both be acknowledged.[24] He says: "Equality is a basic ethical principle, not an assertion of fact."[25] Yet a little further on, when the prescriptive level is addressed, he observes: "The essence of the principle of equal consideration of interests is that we give equal weight in our moral deliberations to the like interests of all those affected by our actions."[26] After all, this means that 'equality' is not only used at the prescriptive stage, but has a descriptive component: 'all those affected' are apparently (in the relevant respect or respects) equal, in order to be considered for equal treatment. When Singer subsequently states "What the principle really amounts to is: an interest is an interest, whoever's interest it may be."[27], this still

[23] R. Posner, "Animal Rights: Legal, Philosophical, and Pragmatic Perspectives", p. 67.
[24] I do not mean to say by this that reason must also necessarily be the decisive element, since I may simply be mistaken, but rather the fact that a descriptive level must be in place before certain behavior is prescribed. Incidentally, in my alternative, prescription does not imply moral prescription, or normativity in that sense.
[25] P. Singer, *Practical Ethics*, p. 20.
[26] P. Singer, *Practical Ethics*, p. 20.
[27] P. Singer, *Practical Ethics*, p. 20.

presupposes (basic) equality. It just means that one abstracts from all traits save the ability to suffer.

I will readily grant that mine is a 'minimalistic' position, and that only the *necessary* conditions for such beings to live peacefully together have been outlined; one may argue that (some of) the obligations towards reasonable beings should also apply to beings that lack reason. This will be discussed in the next section.

3. A realistic perspective

In the previous section, I argued that reason is the feature on the basis of which rights should be granted, and that this feature has also been decisive in realizing legislation to grant and protect rights. This accounts for the different treatment of animals and human beings, the first not being protected in the most basic sense of being killed.[28] For example, I know of no instance in which killing a mosquito is punishable. (Those who consider this example misleading on account of the fact that mosquitoes may be a nuisance or even harmful may exchange it for another animal, to which this does not apply.) Still, it seems I have overlooked an important issue. Is the reason why some animals may be killed or even treated cruelly while others should be left unharmed not simply that the first kind does not suffer, lacking a central nervous system, so that the issue of harming them would be moot in the first place? Perhaps, but that merely

---

[28] There are, admittedly, some exceptions to this rule, laws being in place that protect animals from being treated cruelly, but, first, a lesser sentence applies in being cruel towards an animal than in being cruel towards a human being (*ceteris paribus*), and, second, such legislation is arguably drafted with the interests of human beings in mind (for example, the owners of pets or farm animals, who have an interest in their being protected). The German Constitution provides a clear example from another perspective. Article 20a starts thus: "Der Staat schützt auch in Verantwortung für die künftigen Generationen die natürlichen Lebensgrundlagen und die Tiere…" ("The state protects, mindful also of its responsibility towards future generations, the natural foundations of life and animals…") Animals are obviously (at least partly) considered as means (for future human beings).

specifies the question: do those animals which *are* capable of experiencing harm have natural rights or moral status?

It may be useful to first consider the position of human beings. 'Mankind', or 'humanity', is arguably an invention, a notion to encompass all human beings (without it being always clear what it means to qualify as a human being), so as to reach a stage where divisive characteristics, such as religion, race or gender, are not decisive to be granted certain rights.[29] There does not seem to be a compelling reason, prior to this invention, for those in power to extend the rights to those not in power, and it is not surprising to find such changes realized only (shortly) after the power balance has shifted. In the cases where this was not, or not necessarily, a consideration, such as in the case of the abolition of slavery in the U.S.A., it is clear that one would act inconsistently by allowing conditions one would not oneself find acceptable or agreeable to live under to apply to other beings that are not in the crucial respect or respects different from oneself. In the case of black people being held as slaves, this situation is clear once one realizes that they are rational beings (in the sense of basically rational indicated in the previous section) just as white people are, and that this would be sufficient to grant them the same rights they – i.e., the white people – have established for themselves. The same consideration applies, *mutatis mutandis*, to the extension of suffrage to women, one's gender now acknowledged not to be a relevant characteristic here.

The foregoing analysis does not point to any moral elements, and both the original allotment and the extension of rights may more convincingly be argued

[29] While *homo sapiens* is a species (with the subspecies *homo sapiens sapiens*), determined on the basis of biological criteria, 'mankind' (or 'man', or 'humanity') has become an honorific in law. Biology describes the characteristics of human beings while law prescribes that human beings should be treated in a certain way. Still, the link between being a (human) being and being treated in some way is not evident and, not coincidentally, construed by human beings themselves.

to be based on self-interest. 'Humanity' is not, then, something special on the basis of which rights should be granted or one should be treated in some 'morally acceptable' way. In fact, 'humanity' is such a general, and even vague, word that it hardly has a meaning, or if it has one, it may be linked to, ironically, arbitrary traits, such as the human body; the difficulties a position such as Kateb's faces[30] were indicated in section 1, while reason is not really the decisive characteristic, since mentally handicapped people are fictitiously considered to be reasonable beings, simply because it would apparently be unwelcome or unacceptable not to do so and to treat them as things. It is clear that such a course of action does not constitute a reflection of reality but is rather a moral appeal or a political solution, while I have argued that the former, a moral appeal, is not decisive here.

Those who defend animal rights,[31] or moral treatment of animals,[32] would further abstract and might use 'animality' instead of 'humanity'. Depending on how one deals with matters such as the argument from marginal cases discussed above, 'animality' would be more consistent than 'humanity' (because of the fact just mentioned, that a characteristic such as the human body is obviously no serious candidate to be used as a criterion for some treatment), and in that respect Singer's contribution is valuable. This still raises the question, though, why one should take the interests of animals to heart. Singer maintains: "If a being suffers, there can be no moral justification for refusing to take that suffering into consideration. No matter what the nature of the being, the principle of equality requires that the suffering be counted equally with the like suffering – in so far as

---

[30] Kateb (rightly) dismisses a focus on bodily traits (*Human Dignity*, p. 133), but does not proffer a viable alternative.

[31] E.g. S. Donaldson and W. Kymlicka, *Zoopolis. A Political Theory of Animal Rights*, p. 25: "The basic premise of ART [animal rights theory] is that whenever we encounter [...] vulnerable selves – whenever we encounter 'someone home' – they need protection through the principle of inviolability, which provides a protective shield of basic rights around every individual."

[32] E.g. P. Singer, *Practical Ethics*, p. 50.

rough comparisons can be made – of any other being."[33] What he says is perfectly understandable, but being capable of suffering is merely a criterion to determine whether interests may be relevant: those who may suffer have an interest not to. It does not necessitate those who understand this to abstain from causing their suffering, or to alleviate it. This given does not, in other words, entail the motivation to act in accordance with it. This motivation *is* clear in the case of human beings: allowing harmful behavior would be undesirable as one might oneself fall victim to it and in the most extreme scenario, living together peacefully might cease to be possible.

Supposed animal rights, prior to their being included in man-made law, are no more and no less difficult to substantiate than supposed human rights, and an appeal to acknowledge animal rights on the basis of the fact that human rights exist is nothing other than the extension of a starting point that has not been justified itself.[34]

The foregoing does not necessarily lead to the conclusion that human beings should be allowed to do with animals whatever they want, animals being treated as things in this regard. What was decisive before in forestalling animal rights or some treatment on the basis of supposedly moral considerations, namely self-interest, may now be appealed to in order to prevent this outcome. Self-interest in a narrow sense may not reach this result, for if 'self' is taken to refer only to the person who acts, it may be in one's interest, e.g., to eat meat, while some may even have an urge to harm animals for their enjoyment, the fulfillment of which

[33] P. Singer, *Practical Ethics*, p. 50.

[34] Cf. J. Bentham, *Anarchical Fallacies*, p. 500: "How stands the truth of things? That there are no such things as natural rights – no such things as rights anterior to the establishment of government – no such things as natural rights opposed to, in contradiction to, legal: that the expression is merely figurative; that when used, in the moment you attempt to give it a literal meaning it leads to error, and to that sort of error that leads to mischief – to the extremity of mischief."

would conflict with laws forbidding such behavior. 'Self-interest' may, however, alternatively be taken to extend to a greater domain of subjects, and if animals are considered to be such subjects, there would be sufficient reason to take their interest into consideration.

This use of 'self-interest' may be considered a rhetorical trick, simply utilizing a definition of my own making to reach an outcome that is counter-intuitive. This line of reasoning is not, however, as strange as it may be taken to be. In fact, what has already been said does not deviate from it. I have already pointed out in section 2 that the fiction of rationality is applied to children, 'normal' children being potentially rational, and may be extended to some animals (such as pets) on the basis of the same consideration why it applies to children for some people.[35] I would argue that 'indirect self-interest' is at stake in cases where one's own interest (i.e., 'direct self-interest') is not an issue, while the interest of another being one seeks to serve is relevant, experiencing some bond with that being.[36] Parents make certain, sometimes great, sacrifices for their children. (This consideration applies *a fortiori* to some animal species, although this may be fully contributed to instinctual factors.) Some people may experience a bond with their pets similar to that of children. This does not warrant the same treatment that applies to children (as other considerations apply to the case of children), but it does provide an argument to take their interests seriously.

The foregoing gives rise to two problems. First, a 'popularity contest' may ensue: the cutest or cuddliest animals should be treated well, while other animals, which do not incite feelings of affection, should continue to be treated as mere things. Second, a demarcation line between various sorts of animals seems difficult to

[35] I say 'for some people' because other considerations, discussed in section 2, may be decisive for all people, including those who do not themselves have children.

[36] The demarcation line between direct and indirect self-interest is difficult to draw. I will not explore that issue here.

draw. Perhaps dogs should be protected from harm, but what about, perhaps in descending order of importance, a seagull, a mosquito or an ant?[37] (I have already remarked that the nuisance or harm some animals themselves produce may be a relevant factor.) Both issues may be dealt with from the perspective of those who decide which rights should be granted, and to which beings. Those who make such decisions are those who are basically equal, and, more specifically, basically rational; their interests may, as was indicated, follow from the idea of indirect self-interest. One may on that basis, for example, distinguish between domesticated and non-domesticated animals: "What distinguishes DAs [domesticated animals] from other animals is that we humans have brought them into our society."[38] However, Donaldson and Kymlicka qualify the relationship in terms of duties and the extension of citizenship (to the domesticated animals),[39] and even remark: "[...] domestication makes the extension of citizenship both morally necessary and practically feasible."[40] The latter – the practical feasibility – is defensible, but the substantiation for the former – the moral necessity – is not provided, and may not be forthcoming as the burden of proof may be too great.

In *practical* terms, no great differences need arise between my position and one that starts from moral appeals, and animals themselves will, presumably, not care on what basis they are treated in some way. In both cases, legislation may be implemented on the basis of which animals, or at least some animals, are protected. The underpinnings of such legislation are wanting, however, in the

[37] Taking the interests – or supposed interests – of the latter animals seriously would effectively mean resorting to actions such as those performed by Jains, such as sweeping the ground before walking on it.
[38] S. Donaldson and W. Kymlicka, "Animals and the Frontiers of Citizenship", p. 204.
[39] S. Donaldson and W. Kymlicka, "Animals and the Frontiers of Citizenship", pp. 204, 205.
[40] S. Donaldson and W. Kymlicka, "Animals and the Frontiers of Citizenship", p. 205.

latter case, which is an important reason to exchange it for a more viable alternative, such as the one I have defended.

An approach such as this does not solve the problems mentioned above, and may not even confront others that have remained undiscussed here, but the alternative of clinging to moral terms without their meaning having become apparent, let alone how they might compel one to act in one way rather than another, is less appealing. Should the role of such terms become clear at some point, I would be willing to substitute this alternative for my own position, but it seems safe to say that, at least for now, such a skeptical – or pragmatic – stance is the most acceptable, to which I would add that the desire to be able to make a moral appeal on the basis of natural rights is not the same as the proof of their existence.[41] The same reasoning applies to a moral appeal.[42] If people are motivated, on the basis of indirect self-interest, to end the suffering of (some) animals, it will not be a problem to realize legislation that protects their interests, and such legislation will in that case even be desirable.

Conclusion

It is difficult to maintain that human beings should be granted the most important rights while these should be withheld from animals if one bases one's claim on an account of natural rights or on an ethical theory. It does not follow

---

41 Cf. J. Bentham, *Anarchical Fallacies*, p. 501: "In proportion to the want of happiness resulting from the want of rights, a reason exists for wishing that there were such things as rights. But reasons for wishing there were such things as rights, are not rights; – a reason for wishing that a certain right were established, is not that right – want is not supply – hunger is not bread."

42 Bentham is known for his focus on suffering, relativizing in light of the fact that (some) animals share this ability with human beings the other characteristics (i.e., reason and the – related – ability to speak) that distinguish them (*An Introduction to the Principles of Morals and Legislation*, Ch. 19, p. 143), but this may also be construed as a demonstration of what consequences would follow from a consistent line of reasoning. Bentham's straightforward outlook and his view on morals invite such an interpretation: "The whole difference between politics and morals is this: the one directs the operations of governments, the other directs the operations of individuals; their common object is happiness." (*op. cit.*, Ch. 2, p. 12).

from this discrepancy, however, that animal rights must be acknowledged, as human rights have been acknowledged, for such a basis for human rights is wanting, their defenders' accounts. Arguing that animal rights should be acknowledged as natural rights would only compound to the justification problems natural rights theorists and ethicists face. Still, concluding from this that the opposite result should follow, and that animals should not be protected in any way, attests to an obvious false dilemma, since a third option is available. I have defended such an option, maintaining that rights are generally realized on the basis of self-interest, in the broad sense of indirect self-interest, and that the protection such rights provide may be extended to include (some) animals. The practical results need not significantly differ from those reached on the basis of an approach such as Singer's, but their foundation is arguably more stable, self-interest providing a more solid starting point than a moral appeal.

Made in the USA
Monee, IL
08 November 2026

67814363R10095